SCHAUM'S *Easy* OUTLINES

INTRODUCTION TO PSYCHOLOGY

Other Books in Schaum's Easy Outlines Series Include:

SCHAUM'S *Easy* OUTLINES

INTRODUCTION TO PSYCHOLOGY

BASED ON SCHAUM'S
Outline of Theory and Problems of
Introduction to Psychology, Second Edition
BY ARNO F. WITTIG, Ph.D.

ABRIDGEMENT EDITOR:
LAURA M. SINNETT, Ph.D.

SCHAUM'S OUTLINE SERIES
McGRAW-HILL

New York   Chicago   San Francisco   Lisbon   London   Madrid
Mexico City   Milan   New Delhi   San Juan
Seoul   Singapore   Sydney   Toronto

ARNO F. WITTIG is Professor Emeritus of Psychology and former Dean of the Honors College at Ball State University. He received his B.A. from Hobart College and his M.A. and Ph.D. degrees from The Ohio State University. He has taught introductory psychology for forty years. He specializes in sports psychology research, concentrating on gender differences and psychological rehabilitation from injury. He is a Fellow in three divisions of the American Psychological Association and is the author or coauthor of several books and numerous articles.

LAURA M. SINNETT is Associate Professor of Social-Personality Psychology at Grinnell College in Iowa, where she teaches courses in social psychology and psychology of personality. She received her B.A. from Webster University and her M.S. and Ph.D. degrees from Purdue University. She specializes in emotion research and is the author or coauthor of several conference papers and articles.

7 8 9 DOC DOC 0 9

ISBN 0-07-139882-1

Library of Congress Cataloging-in-Publication Data applied for.

Sponsoring Editor: Barbara Gilson
Editing Supervisor: Maureen B. Walker
Production Supervisors: Tama Harris and Clara Stanley

McGraw-Hill

A Division of The McGraw·Hill Companies

Contents

Chapter 1
PSYCHOLOGY: DEFINITION AND HISTORY

IN THIS CHAPTER:

- ✔ *Definition and Purpose*
- ✔ *Areas of Study*
- ✔ *The Background and Beginning of Psychology*
- ✔ *Early Development of Psychology*
- ✔ *Current Outlooks in Psychology*
- ✔ *Solved Problems*

Definition and Purpose

Psychology is the **scientific study of behavior**. Psychological "behavior" may include actual behaviors, but often "behavior" is a term that is also used to denote cognitive and emotional events. Psychologists try to **describe**, **predict**, and **explain the causes** of animal and human behavior.

Example 1.1 Consider a student who is studying for a psychology course. Reading the text and going over course notes represent behaviors that can be described. Attempting to estimate what the student is likely to do in the future amounts to predicting behavior. Understanding that the student wishes to gain a college degree in psychology provides an explanation for the studying.

Areas of Study

Behavior is defined as any observable or measurable response by a human or animal. Most studies involve human behavior. Animals are studied when the use of human participants would be unethical or impossible and when it is possible to apply findings from animal subjects to human behavior.

Inherited characteristics and **environmental variables** both combine to influence behavior. Although there has been controversy in the history of the field of psychology, most psychologists would agree that both heredity and environmental causes are important—separately and in interaction with each other.

Behaviors may result from **conscious** or deliberate choice. However, some behaviors may result from motives or processes that are below people's levels of awareness. These motives and processes are said to be **unconscious** or **nonconscious**.

Psychology is concerned with both **normal** and **abnormal** behavior. The criteria used to determine abnormality refer to the distress produced by the behavior and the amount of disruption to individual or social functioning produced by the behavior. Such decisions have changed over time and are determined differently across cultures.

Remember

Behavior can be inherited or due to the environment.
Behavior can be conscious or unconscious.
Behavior can be normal or abnormal.

The Background and Beginning of Psychology

Psychology is a relatively new scientific field. Wilhelm Wundt (1832–1920) is credited with founding the discipline of psychology in 1879, the year that he established the first formal psychological laboratory at the University of Leipzig, Germany. Although other researchers had been addressing psychological research questions, Wundt was the first person to refer to psychology—or the study of the psyche/mind—as an independent experimental science. Wundt also began the first scientific journal for psychology and wrote an early physiological psychology textbook.

The field of psychology grew out of a number of disciplines that had been examining questions of a psychological nature. **Philosophy** has traditionally encompassed many concerns of psychologists, such as learning, motivation, personality, and perception. For this reason, many of the first psychology departments at colleges and universities were originally affiliated with philosophy departments. Psychology distinguished itself from philosophy in its emphasis on using the scientific method.

Don't Forget!

Psychology applies the scientific method to the study of behavior.

Methodologies for the scientific study of behavior were adapted from other **sciences**, such as physics, chemistry, and biology. Physics and chemistry originally contributed to the psychological study of sensation and perception. Biology contributed to the psychological study of genetic influences on behavior and to comparative approaches in which the behavior of one species is compared to another.

Medicine contributed to psychology by influencing the way in which abnormal behaviors were conceptualized. Whereas it was common to treat abnormalities as resulting from nonorganic problems, such as possession by evil spirits, the medical community began in the late 1880s to view abnormalities as instances of mental illness. This medical model for abnormality led to the development of psychiatry and, eventually, clinical psychology.

Early Development of Psychology

Early psychology was characterized by the study of **systems** that represented attempts to explain all behavior using a single set of principles. Although no one system is dominant today, contemporary psychology continues to reveal the influences of these early systems approaches.

Structuralism was developed by Wundt, and later by Edward Titchener (1867–1927). The structuralists employed introspection, in which trained subjects attempted to describe stimuli and their own mental processes. It was hoped that these descriptions could provide insight into the structure of the mind and how it worked. The method of introspection was eventually abandoned, primarily because it was impossible to objectively verify individual perceptions.

Functionalism developed in the United States partially in response to the problems of structuralism. Functionalists were influenced by the evolutionary ideas of Charles Darwin, such as species survival and natural selection. Functionalists were concerned with the purposes of behavior and the adaptation or adjustment of people to different environments.

Example 1.2 Current outlooks make use of both structural and functional systems. Physiological psychologists may study different areas or structures of the brain and how they communicate with each other in order to perform many complicated functions.

John Watson (1878–1958) established the field of **behaviorism**, which held that only observable responses were appropriate for scientific study. Behaviorists did not study the mind, because the mind could not be observed. The goal of behaviorism was to identify lawful stimulus-response relationships. Although radical behaviorism has been criticized because psychologists now recognize that some unobservable phenomena are important, the concern with environmental stimuli and resulting behavioral responses has remained important to many contemporary areas of psychology.

Gestalt psychologists working in Germany were concerned with the need to consider an entire perceptual field—a stimulus and its context—in order to understand perceptual issues. They criticized other approaches for fragmenting behavior. The phrase often used to describe the Gestalt position is "the whole is greater than the sum of its parts." Today, perceptual and cognitive psychology make use of Gestalt ideas.

Psychodynamic psychology was developed by Sigmund Freud (1856–1939), a Viennese medical doctor, as a therapeutic technique. Freud believed that early childhood experiences and unconscious motivations and conflicts were important in understanding abnormal behavior. This approach was influential in the formation of clinical, counseling, and developmental psychology.

Current Outlooks in Psychology

Because finding one system to account for all of behavior is highly unlikely, contemporary **perspectives** on psychology focus on more limited areas of study. Still, it is common for current psychologists to approach their work using some ideas from both historical and recent approaches.

Let's Compare . . . ✔

Perspectives	Contributions
Psychodynamic	Unconscious, conflict
Behavioral	Stimuli, responses
Humanistic	Self-actualization
Biological	Physiology
Evolutionary	Genes, natural selection
Cognitive	Mental processes
Sociocultural	Social, cultural influences

Regardless of the perspective adopted, there are many separate fields of psychology that can be broadly categorized as being either **applied** or **experimental** in their approach. Experimental psychology is concerned with explaining the causes of behavior through the use of psychological principles that have been tested, often in laboratory experiments. Applied psychology uses the principles in real-world settings, often with the goal of modifying behavior.

Clinical and **counseling** psychology represent two of the largest applied areas; almost 60 percent of all psychologists in the United States work in these fields. Both clinical and counseling psychologists apply psychological principles to help people overcome problems. Clinicians are more likely to treat or conduct research into abnormal behaviors or mental disorders, while counselors are more likely to work with or conduct research on milder problems, such as selecting a vocation or working on an interpersonal relationship. Whereas clinical or counseling psychologists typically obtain a Ph.D. (doctor of philosophy in psychology) or Psy.D. (doctor of psychology), psychiatrists obtain an M.D. (doctor of medicine). Despite differences in degrees and specific areas of focus, clinicians, counselors, and psychiatrists all attempt to explain problems and treat clients.

Educational psychology applies psychological principles to the enhancement of learning, and may entail an examination of curricula, teaching techniques, or learning facilities. **School** psychology focuses on the assessment and treatment of learning, behavioral, social, or emotional problems that face specific students.

Let's Compare . . . ✔

Fields of Applied Psychology	Areas of Application
Industrial/organizational	Improving productivity in business
Engineering	Equipment design
Consumer	Marketing strategies
Sport	Motivation
Health	Health promoting behaviors
Forensic	Legal practice
Environmental	Effects of crowding

Experimental psychology uses the scientific method (See Chapter 2) to study the principles that explain behavior, often without regard for practical applications. It is common for experimental psychologists to adopt only one of the aforementioned perspectives in their work.

Physiological or **biological** psychologists are concerned with the biological processes that accompany behavior. Some might study how neurotransmitters—brain chemicals that allow for communication among neurons—are related to mental disorders. Others might study topics such as sensation and perception of the physical world, to provide just a couple of examples.

Cognitive psychologists focus on mental processes, such as reasoning, decision making, attention, memory, and retrieval. Computer models of processing information have had a big influence on cognitive psychology.

Developmental psychology deals with change and continuity over the life span of humans. Whereas some developmental psychologists focus on one particular age group, others study topics across age groups. Examples include cognitive, emotional, or social development.

Social psychology examines the influence of the social world on individual and group behavior. Common areas of study include attitudes and persuasion, stereotypes, aggression, helping behavior, and interpersonal relationships.

Example 1.3 Some topics, such as emotion, are approached from many experimental perspectives. Physiological psychologists might study how the amygdala—a particular brain structure—is activated when a person experiences anger. The attention-getting and memorable nature of another's anger could be the focus of a cognitive psychologist. The use of anger to regulate relationships is a concern of social psychologists. Finally, developmental psychologists might work to discover when and how children learn that anger typically is experienced when one person intentionally harms another.

Solved Problems

Solved Problem 1.1 Some research studies involve human subjects; other studies use animals as subjects. Why?

There are several reasons: (1) Sometimes a psychologist is simply interested in learning about animal behavior. (2) Animals are often studied because it would be unethical or impossible to use humans. For example, it is possible to control the breeding of animals so that the contributions of genetic variables to producing behavior can be separated from the contributions of environmental variables. (3) In many cases, the principles governing animal behavior are similar to the principles governing human behavior.

Solved Problem 1.2 What is the relationship between hereditary and environmental influences on a person's behavior?

It is generally accepted that heredity and environment influence behavior individually and that they also interact to jointly produce behavior. As an example of an interaction, a person who is genetically predisposed to enjoy risk-taking behaviors might choose to engage in risky activities and subsequently find them rewarding. Genetic and environmental variables interact in this instance to make it even more likely that the person will engage in risk taking in the future. It is unlikely that the relative amount of each influence can ever be separated, especially in the case of human behavior.

Solved Problem 1.3 What makes applied psychology different from experimental psychology?

The fields of applied psychology are concerned with practical applications of psychological principles. Experimental psychology is more concerned with understanding the principles themselves. To gain this understanding, experimental or scientific psychologists develop theories about human behavior and hypotheses to test their theories.

Chapter 2
METHODOLOGY AND STATISTICS

✔ *Correlation*
✔ *Inferential Statistics*
✔ *Solved Problems*

The Experimental Method

The **experimental method** is a methodology in which a researcher manipulates a variable and measures a response to the manipulated variable, while controlling for extraneous influences that might inappropriately affect the responses. The strength of the experimental method is that it allows researchers to test cause-effect relationships. A **causal relationship** can be assumed if changes in the manipulated variable produce changes in the response variable.

Good research is conducted with **objectivity** at every stage, so that bias is avoided. Research reports are written in enough detail that a skeptical or interested person has sufficient information to **replicate** the experiment and either confirm or disconfirm the original results.

The experimental method is a type of **empirical** study that relies on measurable variables that have **operational definitions**. These definitions refer to the methods used to define or measure the variables.

Psychologists who conduct human and animal research must follow **ethical guidelines** that exist to eliminate or minimize potential harm to research participants. Human participants usually provide **informed consent** to the research procedures before any data are collected. The data that are collected are often **confidentially** or **anonymously** supplied to further protect subjects. Researchers also typically **debrief** participants, giving them a complete explanation of the research once the data have been collected. Research proposals are evaluated for their compliance with ethical guidelines before research can be conducted.

Example 2.1 An experimenter wants to study the effects of room temperature on students' performance. Both room temperature and performance can take on many values; consequently both are variables. The experimenter operationally defines temperature by controlling the degrees Fahrenheit of the room. The researcher records students' scores on an exam as an operational definition of performance.

The Hypothesis

A **hypothesis** is a prediction that is stated in such a way that it can be tested and either confirmed or disconfirmed. Two forms of hypotheses—the null hypothesis and the directional or alternative hypothesis—often are used. The **null hypothesis** states that the manipulations will not result in differences between the performance of the groups being studied. By contrast, the **directional hypothesis** states that the manipulations will alter the performance of the groups. Typically, an experimenter wishes to disconfirm the null hypothesis.

Experimental and Control Groups

Assume that the experimenter in the above example sets out to disconfirm the null hypothesis "Changes in room temperature have no effect on students' exam scores." To test this hypothesis, the experimenter might give the exam in at least three different conditions—once to a group at "normal" room temperature (72°F), once to a group at the "high" (86°F) temperature, and once to a group at the "low" (58°F) temperature.

The normal-temperature group is the **control group**. This group provides a basis for comparison for the two **experimental groups**—the high- and the low-temperature groups.

Independent and Dependent Variables

The **independent variable** is what is manipulated by the experimenter; here, it is temperature. The response that is presumed to be caused or influenced by the independent variable is the **dependent variable**. In this example, exam scores are the dependent variable.

Remember

Dependent variables **depend** on or are caused by independent variables.

Extraneous and Confounding Variables

Extraneous variables are irrelevant to the experimenter's purpose, but they may influence the behavior of the experimental and control groups nonetheless. **Confounding variables** are also irrelevant, but they influence the behavior of only one of the groups. Both types of variables should be eliminated or minimized so that a subject's response is caused only by the effect of the independent variable.

Example 2.2 In the "temperature-exam" study, noise could be an extraneous variable. It should be held constant for all groups. If the women students were assigned to one group and the men students were assigned to another group, then gender would be a confound. If these extraneous and confounding variables were not eliminated, the experimenter would not be able to conclude that exam scores were influenced by room temperature.

Sampling

Sampling is a method used to select members of each group so that each is an equal and accurate representation of the **population**, the entire group from which subjects may be chosen.

The most common form of sampling is **random sampling**, in which each member of a population has an equal chance of being selected, as if numbers were drawn from a hat. This can be accomplished by assigning random numbers to each population member. The experimenter chooses subjects until a large enough sample has been chosen. Occasionally, a researcher may believe that certain subgroups should be equally represented in each of the experimental and control groups. In such cases, the researcher may employ **stratified** or **matched sampling**, so that each group has the same number of subjects of each type, for example, men and women.

Once subjects are randomly selected from a population, they need to be **randomly assigned** to the experimental and control groups. This is done so that each subject has an equal chance of being in each group.

Experimenter Bias

Two common forms of, often unintentional, experimenter bias are **demand characteristics** and **expectancy effects**. The experimenter may anticipate certain responses from subjects and elicit or demand these anticipated responses through subtle means. Alternatively, the experimenter may interpret the behavioral information in a manner that fulfills his or her expectancy. Methods to eliminate experimenter bias include not informing participants about the hypotheses (**single-blind control**) and not informing both participants and those who are actually collecting the data about the hypotheses (**double-blind control**).

Other Psychological Methodologies

When the experimental method cannot be used, psychologists rely on other techniques to gather data. Although these techniques can provide valuable information, they prohibit the experimenter from making causal conclusions as is possible with an experiment.

Naturalistic observations occur when researchers simply record existing behaviors in an unmanipulated context.

Example 2.3 Observing similar behaviors in people randomly selected from two different cultures can provide cross-cultural research information. Because culture cannot be ethically manipulated, cross-cultural data always result from naturalistic observations.

Clinical or counseling psychologists often conduct **case studies**, in which the problems, insights, and techniques important in treating a person are recorded. These **clinical case histories** can be studied by others interested in learning about particular factors that may be important in understanding behavior.

Psychologists also often obtain behavioral information by asking subjects to respond to specially designed **tests**, **surveys**, **interviews**, or **questionnaires**. These instruments have been designed to investigate many aspects of behavior, including personality, intelligence, and attitudes. Their advantages are that they allow for efficient data gathering and they allow for easy comparisons of the performance of one subject with the performance of others. A disadvantage is that real-life behavior may differ from self-reported behavior.

Statistics

Statistics are used to analyze, interpret, and present numerical data. The value of statistics is that they can provide simplified descriptions of the data and they permit inferences to be made from the data provided by the sample to the entire population from which the sample was selected. These two uses of statistics are known as **descriptive** and **inferential statistics**, respectively.

Certain symbols have universal meaning in statistical formulas. Some of the most common symbols common are:

$$N = \text{number of scores}$$
$$X = \text{score or scores}$$
$$M \text{ or } \bar{X} = \text{mean or average score}$$
$$d = \text{difference of a score from the mean}$$
$$\Sigma = \text{sum of}$$
$$D = \text{difference in rank}$$
$$r \text{ or } \rho = \text{correlation}$$
$$SD \text{ or } \sigma = \text{standard deviation}$$

Example 2.4 These symbols are used together. Thus, the formula

$$M = \frac{\Sigma X}{N}$$

would be read: The mean is equal to the sum of the scores divided by the number of scores.

Frequency Distributions

Frequency distributions are used to represent data. By convention, the independent variable is plotted on the **abscissa** (x-axis), and the dependent variable is plotted on the **ordinate** (y-axis). Frequency distributions are drawn by dividing the measurement scale of the independent variable into class intervals, so that each datum will fall within one of the class intervals, depending on the value of the independent variable.

Frequency polygons present the data as line graphs; **frequency histograms** present the data as bar graphs. **Symmetrical distributions** have an equal number of scores on each side of the middle of the distribution.

Skewed distributions are those in which scores are concentrated at one end. The frequency histogram below is fairly symmetrical.

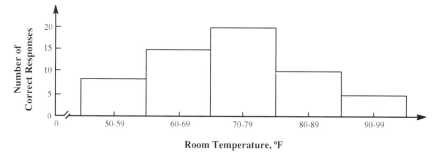

Figure 2-1 A symmetrical frequency histogram of room temperature data.

Measures of Central Tendency

A **measure of central tendency** uses a single number to summarize a group of scores.

The **mean** is determined by summing all the scores and dividing the sum by the number of scores. The formula for the mean appears in Example 2.4. The mean is influenced by extreme or outlying scores. For this reason, other measures of central tendency may be desirable.

The **median** is the middle score, or the point below (and above) which 50 percent of the scores in a distribution fall. This is also referred to as the **50th percentile** of the distribution.

The most frequently occurring score is the **mode**. Unlike the mean and the median, the mode can be represented by two numbers.

Measures of Variability

Variability refers to the dispersion of scores around the measure of central tendency. The **range** is easily calculated by subtracting the value of the lowest score from the value of the highest score. The **standard deviation** (*SD*) is a better measure of variability because it is not influenced by outlying scores, as is the range. The *SD* can be calculated as follows:

$$SD = \sqrt{\frac{\sum d^2}{N}}$$

Example 2.5 On a 20-item quiz, suppose seven students get the scores listed below. The calculation of the *SD* would progress as follows:

Score (*X*)	Difference from the Mean (*d*)	d^2
17	$17-13=4$	16
16	$16-13=3$	9
14	$14-13=1$	1
13	$13-13=0$	0
12	$12-13=-1$	1
12	$12-13=-1$	1
7	$7-13=-6$	36

$\sum X = 91$
$N = 7$
$M = 13$

$$SD = \sqrt{\frac{\sum d^2}{N}} = \sqrt{\frac{64}{7}} = \sqrt{9.14} = 3.024$$

The Normal Probability Distribution

Many scores plotted on a graph often fall in a nearly symmetrical bell-shaped distribution known as the **normal curve**. This is a graphic representation of the **normal probability distribution**, an idealized example of which appears in Figure 2-2. About 68 percent of a set of scores fall between the mean plus or minus one *SD*. About 95 percent fall between the mean plus or minus two *SD*s.

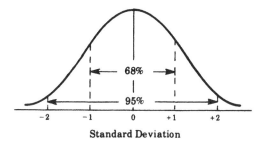

Figure 2-2 An idealized normal probability distribution.

Using the normal curve, it is possible to calculate a **percentile** value for a given score. The percentile refers to the percentage of scores in a distribution that falls below a given score. For example, the mean score represents the 50th percentile (also the median), and a score that is one *SD* above the mean is at the 84th percentile [50 + ½ (68)]. Any score can be located within the normal probability distribution and thus compared with other scores, if the mean and *SD* are known.

Correlation

The **coefficient of correlation** represents the linear relationship between two variables. Correlations range between −1 and +1. A negative correlation indicates that the variables are negatively related, so that as the value of one increases, the value of the other decreases. A positive correlation indicates that both variables rise together. Correlations that approach 0 indicate that the variables are only weakly, if at all, related.

Example 2.6 The **scatter diagram** in Figure 2-3 represents a plot of the results of the time needed to run a mile as a function of the average number of hours of weekly training of each person tested. The scatter diagram indicates a negative correlation of about −.67, so that the greater the number of hours of training, the less time is needed to complete a mile run.

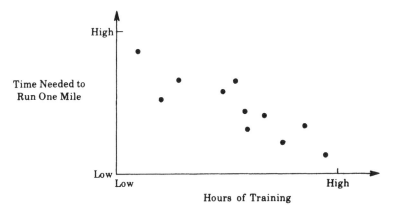

Figure 2-3 A scatter diagram.

A correlation does not automatically indicate a causal relationship between two variables. When there is evidence to support a causal interpretation, the statistical technique of **regression** is used to indicate the strength of the causal relationship between the two variables.

Inferential Statistics

Predictions about the behavior of a population from which a sample was drawn form the basis of **inferential statistics**. Such results are described in terms of **statistical significance**. Arbitrarily, psychologists define a statistically significant result as one that could occur by chance less than 5 times in 100, were the experiment repeated an infinite number of times. This is often written as $p < .05$.

Solved Problems

Solved Problem 2.1 If a psychologist was interested in investigating attitudes about a social problem in different neighborhoods of a city, how might the sampling be done?

Once the geographic boundaries of the neighborhood are determined, **random sampling** would
mean that every person within any one neighborhood would have an equal chance of being selected as a representative of that neighborhood. If the
psychologist believes that it is significant that the
person is a home owner versus a renter, then it
might be necessary to determine the percentages of each in each neighborhood and then select subjects accordingly. This would be a **stratified
sample**.

Solved Problem 2.2 Suppose you have a normal probability distribution
with $SD = 10$ and the value of the score at the 84th percentile $= 90$. What
is the mean of the distribution?

Using the normal curve, you can determine that 90 is 1 SD above the
mean. Subtracting the SD of 10 from 90 provides the mean of 80.

Chapter 3
BIOLOGICAL FOUNDATIONS

In This Chapter:

- ✔ *Elements of a Neuron*
- ✔ *Transmission of a Signal*
- ✔ *Organization of the Nervous System*
- ✔ *The Glandular Systems*
- ✔ *Solved Problems*

Elements of a Neuron

A **neuron** is a single cell that contains a cell body (with the cell nucleus), dendrites, and an axon. There are billions of neurons in the human body that are bunched together to form nerves. Neurons carry signals throughout the body.

The **cell body** (or soma) is the center of a neuron. A neuron's cell body has two different types of branches—dendrites and an axon.

Dendrites, which are short and thin, form the receiving function of a neuron. They receive neurotransmitter signals (see the next section) that have been sent by other neurons. If enough excitatory messages are received, a neural signal is transmitted through the length of a cell as an impulse.

A single **axon**, with branches called **terminal buttons** at its end, projects from the cell body. The axon conducts the neural impulse away from the cell body to the end of the axon, which then passes the signal to the dendrites of nearby neurons. Axons vary in length, from microns to feet, depending on their location. Many axons are covered with **myelin**, a fatty substance that facilitates signal conduction.

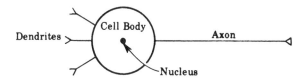

Figure 3-1 A simplified illustration of a neuron.

Transmission of a Signal

The process of **neural transmission** requires that neural signals travel the length of a cell and then cross a gap to activate the next cell, where the process is repeated.

A signal first reaches a cell when a **neurotransmitter** that is secreted by the axon of one cell crosses a **synapse**, or gap, between the axon and the dendrite of the next cell. The synapse is a one-way connection, with transmission going from one cell's axon to another cell's dendrites (or occasionally its cell body or axon), but not in the reverse direction.

The terminal button at the end of each axon contains **synaptic vesicles** that hold a neurotransmitter. As the signal reaches the end of an axon, the vesicles release the neurotransmitter, which is then picked up by the dendrites of nearby cells.

Neurotransmitters interact chemically with the cell membrane of the next neuron by "fitting into" receptors on the dendrites of the receiving cell. Neurotransmitters may excite or inhibit the firing of the receiving cell. The **graded potential** of the cell refers to the sum of the **excitatory** and **inhibitory impulses**. If these exceed a cell's firing threshold, the cell is activated and transmits an electrical signal throughout its length.

Example 3.1 Neurotransmission is like putting together the pieces of a large jigsaw puzzle. Pieces of a puzzle are shaped differently, as are neurotransmitter molecules. A puzzle is completed only when the correctly shaped pieces are put into place. Similarly, neurotransmission occurs only when particular neurotransmitters literally "fit" into receptors on the dendrites of the receiving cells.

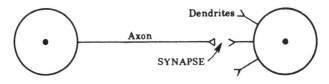

Figure 3-2 An illustration of a synaptic gap. The synaptic gap means that there is no direct contact between the axon of the "sending" cell and the dendrite of the "receiving" cell. The neural signal is carried across the synaptic gap by a neurotransmitter released by the axon.

You Need to Know ✔

Neurotransmitter types	What they do
Endorphins (natural opiates)	Regulate pain, pleasure
Dopamine	Regulates attention, movement, learning
Serotonin	Regulates sleep, arousal, mood

In a resting state, the cell membrane of a neuron maintains a certain level of permeability in which the inside of the cell is slightly negative in its electrical charge compared to the outside. This is the **resting potential** of the neuron. It exists because of the location of positively and negatively charged ions both outside and inside a cell.

When the graded potential exceeds the firing threshold, the signal passes down the length of the cell as an **action potential** in an all-or-none (the cell either fires or it does not) fashion. As the permeability of the axon membrane nearest the cell body changes quickly, the electrical charges reverse (the inside of the cell becomes positive, and the outside becomes negative). This is called **depolarization**. Repolarization occurs quickly as adjoining cell locations are depolarized, until the signal has traveled the length of the axon.

The **refractory phase** is the time required for cell repolarization. Although it is very short (less than one millisecond), no signal can be transmitted during the first part of this time—the **absolute refractory period**. The rest of the time—the **relative refractory period**—the cell can again be activated, but only if excitation is stronger than normal.

The action potential is the same intensity every time a neuron fires. Signal strength depends on the frequency of a neuron's firing and the number of neurons that fire.

> Communication between different cells is chemical.
> Communication within any one cell is electrical.

Organization of the Nervous System

The **central nervous system (CNS)** contains the brain and the spinal cord, which are joined at the base of the brain to allow for signals to pass between the brain and body. Both receive sensory messages from the **afferent** (sensory) part of the peripheral nervous system (see below) and send signals via the **efferent** (motor and autonomic) part of the peripheral nervous system. The spinal cord is involved in brain-body communication and the control of reflexes; the brain controls more sophisticated functions, such as perception, memory, and breathing.

The brain has three major anatomic regions or layers. The first is the **hindbrain**, which includes the medulla, pons, cerebellum, and reticular formation. The **medulla** controls heartbeat, circulation, breathing, chewing, and salivation. The **pons** controls sleep and movement. Movement and balance are controlled by the **cerebellum**. The **reticular formation** is involved in attention and arousal. These basic survival functions and structures vary little across different species.

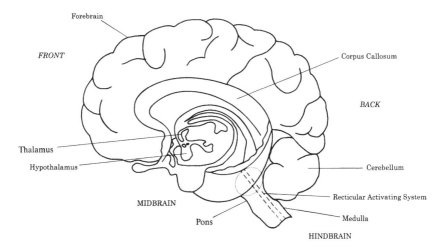

Figure 3-3 The layers and structures of the brain.

The **midbrain** is located above the hindbrain. It handles all sensory information that passes between the spinal cord and the forebrain. The midbrain is also involved in body movement in response to auditory and visual information.

The third and most highly evolved layer of the brain is the **forebrain**, which contains the limbic system and the two cerebral hemispheres. The **limbic system** consists of the thalamus, hypothalamus, hippocampus, amygdala, and septum. The **thalamus** processes and relays sensory information to the forebrain. The **hypothalamus** regulates survival behaviors, such as eating, drinking, and sexual activity, as well as the body's internal environment. The **pituitary gland** is also regulated by the hypothalamus (see below). The **hippocampus** and **amygdala** are involved in memory and emotion. Pleasure is related to the **septum**.

The outer layer of the **cerebral hemispheres** is the **cerebral cortex**, which controls complex mental skills. The **central** and **lateral fissures** are two especially deep convolutions on the cortical surface that help define the four cortical lobes (**frontal**, **parietal**, **occipital**, **temporal**) on each hemisphere.

The **corpus callosum** is a thick band of fibers that connect the right and left hemispheres. These fibers provide a pathway for signals to pass from one side to the other.

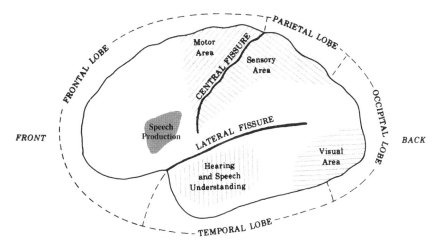

Figure 3-4 The cerebral cortex. This illustration provides labels for the different functions that have been associated with different areas of the cerebral hemispheres. Although much of the brain is relatively unmapped, it is likely that association, memory, and other cognitive abilities are located in the cerebral hemispheres, especially in the frontal lobes.

Plasticity refers to the adaptations of the brain. Increased dendritic branching due to practice, activity, and some medications is likely responsible for plasticity.

Traditional methods of evaluating the structural location of brain activity include observing behavioral changes after trauma to specific brain structures and using an **electroencephalograph (EEG)** to measure electrical impulses that result from performing particular activities, such as dreaming.

Recent and more sophisticated methods involve using **computer-**

ized axial tomography (CAT scan) which relies on x-ray images of tissue density, positron emission tomography (PET scan) which assesses glucose metabolism, thereby indicating particularly active regions of the brain, magnetic resonance imaging (MRI) and superconducting quantum interference devices (SQUID), both of which provide structural and functional information by assessing differences in the magnetic field throughout the brain.

The peripheral nervous system (PNS) includes the sympathetic and parasympathetic portions of the autonomic nervous system and the somatic system, which is extensively discussed in Chapter 5.

The sympathetic system is involved in aroused or excited activity. It consists of nerve fibers linked to the thoracic and lumbar (middle) portions of the spinal cord and visceral organs. The parasympathetic system operates antagonistically, or opposite to the sympathetic system. The parasympathetic nerve fibers are related to quiet, recuperative functions; they are located in the cervical (top) and sacral (bottom) portions of the spinal cord.

The Glandular Systems

Two glandular systems are important for the body. The exocrine glands secrete fluids to outer surfaces of the body, while the endocrine glands secrete hormones, or chemical messengers, throughout the bloodstream to "target" organs or glands.

The pituitary gland or "master gland," is connected to the hypothalamus—providing an important nervous system and endocrine system link. It is responsible for such behaviors as stress reactions, physical growth, and the actions of other endocrine glands.

Thyroxin, secreted by the thyroid gland, regulates metabolism and is related to motivation and mood. The adrenal glands secrete adrenaline and noradrenaline, which operate antagonistically to regulate mood, emotion, blood pressure, and blood sugar levels. The gonads secrete hormones that control sexual development and activity.

Solved Problems

Solved Problem 3.1 Why are psychologists interested in the biological foundations of behavior?

Often, practical applications of physiological information can help psychologists to predict and control behavior. For instance, appetite difficulties may result from a malfunction of the hypothalamus, while damage to the occipital lobe of the brain may be associated with the development of blind spots in the visual field.

Solved Problem 3.2 Brain mapping indicates that sensory functions are located in the cerebral hemispheres. Does this mean that the somatic nervous system does not sense stimuli?

The somatic part of the PNS does receive and transmit sensory signals, but the interpretation of the signals is made in the CNS. This indicates how areas of the brain work together to perform many tasks.

Chapter 4
DEVELOPMENTAL PSYCHOLOGY

Genetics

Genetics is the study of the biological transmission of characteristics from parents to offspring that takes place at conception when the male's sperm unites with the female's ovum (the **germ cells**) to form a **zygote**. The zygote repeatedly divides, resulting in a multicellular organism.

One set of 46 **chromosomes** (23 pairs) is contained in all human cells (except the germ cells which contain 23 single chromosomes). Chromosomes are contributed by each parent through the sperm and ovum.

One particular pair of chromosomes determines the biological sex of the offspring. Females have an XX set and males have an XY set. These pairs randomly split in germ cells. All eggs carry an X chromosome, but sperm are equally likely to carry an X or a Y. The sex of a child is determined by which particular sperm cell (an X or a Y) happens to fertilize an ovum first.

Genes are found on a long molecule called **deoxyribonucleic acid (DNA)**, which is organized into chromosomes when combined with a protein structure. Genes, which are also paired, are the basic unit of hereditary transmission. Genes direct the production of proteins, which determines how an organism will develop. Rarely, a change occurs in the DNA so that a cell does not replicate exactly. This is a **mutation**, which is permanent and often harmful.

The presence or absence of various genes in a zygote determines characteristics. Sometimes characteristics depend on one or two genes; more often characteristics are determined by many genes. This total genetic pattern is the **genome**.

Each pair of genes is made up of **dominant** and **recessive genes**. If a pair contains both types, then the dominant gene will determine a characteristic. Recessive genes manifest themselves only when both genes on a pair are recessive.

Example 4.1 Eye color may be either brown (B below; determined by a dominant gene) or blue (b below; recessive gene). Offspring will have blue eyes only if both parents transmit the recessive gene in the germ cells that form the zygote, even if both parents have brown eyes, as is shown in the figure below. There is a 25 percent chance of this occurring and a 75 percent chance that offspring will have brown eyes. Furthermore, 25 percent of offspring will have only the dominant BB combination and thus will always produce brown eyed offspring.

FATHER

		B	b
MOTHER	B	BB	Bb
	b	Bb	bb

Figure 4-1 **The genetic transmission of eye color**.

Birth defects are either a result of a defective gene or the influence of an environmental agent during pregnancy. **Genetic counseling** by professionals can determine the probabilities of genetic defects before or during pregnancy. **Gene therapy** offers the possibility of correcting genetic defects by introducing healthy genes into existing cells.

Example 4.2 An environmental agent that affects the development of offspring is alcohol. **Fetal alcohol syndrome** results in slow mental and physical growth in children whose mothers consumed large amounts of alcohol during pregnancy.

Example 4.3 Huntington's disease is an inherited neurodegenerative disorder determined by a single gene and revealed by a genetic test. A person with this gene can expect symptoms of erratic movement after age 40 and death within about 15 years of that. There is a 50 percent chance of passing on the Huntington's gene to the next generation.

 Did You Know?

- Identical twins have the same genetic pattern because they result from one zygote or conception.
- Fraternal twins are no more alike than any two siblings because they result from two zygotes or conceptions.

Selective breeding is an attempt to produce desirable characteristics in offspring by controlling the mating of parents with particular characteristics. This has been used to produce pedigreed dogs, cats, racehorses, and cattle. **Eugenics** refers to producing humans through selective breeding, a practice that is not accorded much respect because of the impossibility of determining what characteristics are desirable.

The study of the relative influences of heredity (**nature**) and environment (**nurture**) on behavior is called **behavioral genetics**. **Heritability** is the proportion of the variation of a characteristic among a population (not an individual) that can be attributed to heredity.

Example 4.4 Investigations using twins, siblings, and other relatives can estimate the effects of hereditary and the environment on certain behaviors. Common study designs include using identical and fraternal twins who were separated at birth and raised in different environments (versus those who were not separated). Studies find that the greater the proportion of genetic characteristics shared by the children, the higher the correlation in their behaviors, whether they were raised together or apart. However, even two unrelated children who appear similar are more likely to be treated similarly than are those who appear different. This finding indicates how difficult it can be to accurately estimate the relative effects of heredity and environment on behavior.

Evolution and Genetics

Evolution is the change in a species that occurs gradually, over many generations. Charles Darwin's *The Origin of the Species* (1859) was the first study of evolution. His idea was that characteristics that enhance **adaptation**, and consequently survival, are more likely to be passed on to successive generations than are characteristics that are not adaptive. This adaptation of offspring eventually serves to increase the survival of a species (e.g., "survival of the fittest").

Ethology is the study of the behavior of organisms in their natural habitats. Some behavioral patterns are **species-specific**, meaning that the pattern is common to all members of that species only. **Instincts** are species-specific behaviors that are predispositions to a pattern of behavior that is controlled by hereditary factors.

 **Note!**

Although instincts are hereditary or innate, they are usually modified or triggered by the environment.

Imprinting is an example of an instinct that involves some learning. Many birds, such as ducklings, will follow moving objects soon after hatching. Usually this is the mother. But if the mother is not present, the ducklings will follow other moving objects, such as a researcher.

Physical Development

Human **prenatal** development is divided into three periods: the **germinal**, **embryonic**, and **fetal stages**.

Let's Compare ... ✔

Stage	Ages	Developmental Events
Germinal	1 to 2 Weeks	Zygote begins mitosis (cell division); implants in wall of uterus
Embryonic	Weeks 3 to 8	Cell division continues; recognizable features
Fetal	Weeks 9 to 38	Grows to 18 to 21 inches and about 7 pounds; viable at about 28 weeks

Postnatal development is from birth until death. The sequence of development includes infancy, childhood, adolescence, and adulthood. Although these labels imply that development proceeds in stages, it is actually a continuous process that is studied using particular research methods and principles.

Longitudinal studies are conducted over a long time span using the same subjects. **Cross-sectional studies** are conducted over a short time using subjects of different age groups. Both designs provide useful information. Although longitudinal studies are costly and often have high dropout rates, they do hold heredity constant and allow one to study the effects of early experiences on later development.

Deprivation refers to a reduction in stimulation levels or opportunities that produces below normal development. **Enrichment** is an enhancement of stimulation or opportunities resulting in above normal development. A **critical period** is a portion of developmental time in which deprivation or enrichment is most likely to have effects.

Example 4.5 Critical periods are found in many aspects of human development. Second language acquisition is much easier to accomplish if started before puberty rather than later for reasons that are not yet understood. This also illustrates the importance of understanding cultural influences on development. Children in countries outside the United States are encouraged to acquire a second language early in their schooling, unlike children in the United States.

Physical development occurs in a head-to-toe (**cephalo-caudal trend**) and center-to-outside (**proximo-distal trend**) fashion. Although physical development is influenced by environmental variables, such as nutrition, the sequence of development is the same for all humans. There are **individual differences** in growth rates (and in social and cognitive development) that vary from the statistical norms.

Physical markers denote significant changes. **Puberty**, the point at which the sexual organs mature, signifies the start of adolescence. Early adulthood is characterized by peak physical performance. **Menopause** is marked by the cessation of menstrual periods and fertility in women. Reductions in hearing, vision, reaction times, and strength mark older adulthood. The progressive brain disorder, **Alzheimer's disease**, is experienced primarily in older age.

Cognitive Development

Perceptual development refers to the integration, interpretation, and understanding of sensory stimuli. Perceptual development occurs even in neonates, as measured by such behaviors as changes in heart rate, sucking behavior, and facial imitation responses, and it continues throughout the formative years (see Chapter 5).

Language acquisition occurs through an invariant sequence of language development, which is similar for all languages. This sequence is marked by cooing, babbling, one-word utterances, short "telegraphic speech" patterns, longer phrases, longer sentences, and finally, by about age 4, speech patterning similar to that of adults.

Swiss psychologist **Jean Piaget** (1896–1980) was an influential researcher who proposed a fixed sequence of stages of **cognitive development**. Although his stages have been questioned, and in some cases refuted, his work has been important in prompting further study of cognitive development. The stages appear below.

Piaget's Stages of Cognitive Development

Stage	*Age* (*Years*)	*Learning*
Sensorimotor	0–2	Difference between self and objects; influence of action on environment; object permanence
Preoperational	2–7	Language; use of numbers; classification of objects; conservation principle
Concrete operational	7–11	Logical thought; development of relational ideas; focus on concrete or observable objects
Formal operational	Over 11	Abstract thought; reason via hypotheses; concern for future and ideological issues

Piaget relied on the concepts of **assimilation** (incorporating new material into a **schema** or existing knowledge) and **accommodation** (modification of existing schema to include new information) in describing learning. Also, his theory tended to downplay the amount of cognitive development that occurs in favor of emphasizing the sequence of stages of development.

The **information-processing approach** provides an alternative conception of cognitive development. In this approach, cognitive development is active and marked by increases in language, verbal fluency, numerical skills, knowledge, problem solving, and proficiency in applying these to various circumstances. Information-processing theories emphasize continual changes in the efficiency of processing information rather than a fixed sequence of stages of development.

Social Development

Social development is marked by **integration**, the connection to society through relationships and responsibilities, and **differentiation**, the formation of a separate social identity.

Attachment is the development of a positive, close emotional bond between a caregiver and an infant that indicates the initial phase of social development. The child's link to the caregiver strengthens during the first year of life, to the point where **separation anxiety** may be displayed when the caregiver leaves the child. Separation anxiety does not result in negative consequences.

Peer-group influence serves an increasingly important role in social development. By age 2, children are more self-reliant and likely to interact with peers. With age, play becomes less egocentric and more interactive, thereby fostering an understanding of others, the development of physical and social control, and the capacity to respond appropriately. Children also learn **role taking**, or the ability to understand another person's point of view.

 **Note!**

- Gender roles are the behaviors, traits, and values considered appropriate for males and females.
- Gender roles are learned from others and vary considerably over time and across cultures.

Morality is based on learning what is viewed as right and wrong by a particular culture. Lawrence Kohlberg applied the stage ideas of Piaget to **moral development**. During his first stage of moral development, the **preconventional** stage, behavior is governed by punishments and rewards. Others' expectations for behavior determine the basis for morality in the second, **conventional** stage. Kohlberg called the third stage **postconventional**, with behaviors determined by universal, abstract principles of justice.

Carol Gilligan criticized Kohlberg's work because it was based exclusively on research with males. She proposed an alternative **morality of care** or compassion that might be more typical of females. Although research has not fully supported Gilligan's ideas, they do provide a more complete view of moral reasoning.

Life span development has not received as much attention as childhood has. The best known work is that of Erik Erikson's stage theory of **identity formation**, in which he posits a particular psychosocial crisis to be addressed at each stage of development.

Erikson's Stages of Psychosocial Development

Stage	Age (Years)	Crisis Condition
1. Trust v. mistrust	0–1	Relationship with caregiver, satisfaction of basic needs v. lack of care, deprivation
2. Autonomy v. shame, doubt	2–3	Support, permission for learning v. lack of support, overprotection
3. Initiative v. guilt	4–5	Encouragement of exploration, independent behavior v. lack of encouragement
4. Industry v. inferiority	6–11	Training for mastery of social, school skills v. poor training, lack of support
5. Identity v. role confusion	12–20	Establishing unique social roles v. confusion of identity, purpose

6. Intimacy v. isolation	20–40	Warm, interactive relationships v. loneliness
7. Generativity v. self-absorption	40–65	Purpose, productivity, sense of contribution v. lack of success, regression
8. Integrity v. despair	Over 65	Fulfillment, acceptance of life v. disgust, dissatisfaction

Other work has focused on **dying** and **death**. Elisabeth Kubler-Ross proposed a five-stage model to describe the challenges associated with facing death. The stages are: **denial**, **anger**, **bargaining**, **depression**, and **acceptance**. Research indicates that all of these stages are commonly experienced, although not necessarily in this order.

Solved Problems

Solved Problem 4.1 How does the study of evolution differ from the study of genetics? Why are psychologists interested in evolution?

Genetics is the study of the transfer of characteristics from one generation to the next. Evolution looks at gradual changes in species that occur over long periods and involve many generations.

Understanding evolution helps psychologists comprehend the sources of human behavior. Humans have developed unique patterns of behavior in the same way they have developed unique patterns of physiological characteristics. These patterns are species-specific and are comparable to the behavior patterns found in other species.

Solved Problem 4.2 The directors of a community preschool program wish to help adults recognize situations that encourage and hinder child development. They enlist a developmental psychologist to speak about deprivation and enrichment. What would be the points of the talk?

Deprivation means "doing without," and research has shown that depriving children of opportunities usually results in an incomplete or reduced level of accomplishment. All children should be supported so that motor, cognitive, and social skills develop. For example, the psychologist may suggest that "baby talk" not be used so that children learn from models using standard language.

More than minimal support may be beneficial. This environmental enrichment may result in enhanced developmental accomplishments. Although heredity may place some limits on developed characteristics, the benefits of enrichment are clear. For example, storytelling can give children opportunities to develop their verbal skills.

Chapter 5
SENSATION AND PERCEPTION

IN THIS CHAPTER:

✔ *Basic Sensory Processes*
✔ *Signal Detection Theory*
✔ *Types of Sensory Processes*
✔ *Perception: External Cues*
✔ *Perception: Internal Cues*
✔ *Unusual Perceptual Experiences*
✔ *Solved Problems*

Sensation is the process by which stimuli are detected, identified, and gauged. Sensation merely reveals or conveys information, while **perception** is the **interpretation** of the information. It is actually more appropriate to identify seven, rather than five, basic senses: vision, audition, smell, taste, touch—cutaneous or skin (based on outside signals), equilibrium, and kinesthesis (based on internal states).

Basic Sensory Processes

Psychophysics is the study of basic sensory processes that concern the physical nature of stimuli and the evoked responses. A certain sequence of events is necessary for every sense to operate. An appropriate stimulus must be of sufficient strength. The signal is picked up by a **receptor**

(a specialized nerve ending) and transmitted through the sensory (or somatic) peripheral nervous system to the brain. The signal activates a part of the brain that records the signal as a sensation. Most sensory receptors are in well-protected portions of the body.

Note!

Stimuli outside an organism's range of reception are not detected. This is why dog whistles are heard by dogs but not by humans.

Stimulation must be of sufficient strength for reception to occur. This is called a **threshold**. The **absolute threshold** is the point at which the presence of a stimulus is detected 50 percent of the time. The **difference threshold** (or the **just noticeable difference**, or **jnd**) is the minimum change in a stimulus that can be detected. The relationship between the value of the original stimulus and the amount of change needed to be noticed is known as **Weber's law**.

Example 5.1 If it takes a 1-inch increase in the diameter of a 20-inch diameter circle to be noticed, Weber's law predicts that a 2-inch change is needed when the original diameter is 40 inches. Thus, a small change in noise will be noticed in a quiet environment, while a greater change will be needed to be recognized in a noisy room.

Humans appear to be able to make adjustments and adopt a pattern of behavior that allows them to cope with an unusual level of stimulation, a process known as **sensory adaptation**.

When a stimulus is picked up by a receptor, its energy is changed into an action potential that begins the sequence of events leading to the brain's registration of the sensation. This change is called the **transduction** of the signal.

Signal Detection Theory

Signal detection theory has shown that some early sensory concepts were naïve. Absolute threshold values and jnds may vary, depending on a number of conditions. **Motivational variables** can affect a person's judgment about the presence or absence of a stimulus or a change in the stimulus level. Analysis of such situations is based on all the possible outcomes (see Example 5.2).

Example 5.2 Signal detection theory arose in part from concerns during World War II. Sailors had to decide whether enemy submarines were nearby. If a submarine was nearby and a sailor noted this by activating the alarm for "battle stations," this was a hit. If there was no submarine and the sailor sounded no alarm, a correct reject occurred. However, if no submarine was present but the sailor saw an iceberg and mistakenly believed a submarine was present, sounding the alarm represented a false alarm. The more serious error happened when a submarine was present and the sailor missed it. Making no response placed the ship in danger and constituted a miss. In such circumstances, the relative payoffs and costs favored sounding the alarm whenever the possibility existed that an enemy submarine was in the area.

Extraneous stimuli also influence the stimulus recognition process. Such irrelevant stimuli often are classified as **noise**. Excesses of noise may raise threshold values by making it more difficult to detect the appropriate stimulus (e.g., the "noise" of the iceberg, in Example 5.2).

Past experience provides information regarding the likelihood that a stimulus will occur in the future. With a great likelihood, a person may detect the stimulus, whereas a very small likelihood means the person may devote his or her energies to other stimuli. Organisms raised in restricted circumstances are less likely to recognize a stimulus occurrence than are those raised in normal situations, thus illustrating the importance of signal detection theory for perceptual development.

You Need to Know

Sensitivity to certain kinds of stimuli is hardwired as a result of hereditary or evolutionary development. For example, chickens will seek shelter when a hawk flies over, even if they see only the hawk's shadow.

Types of Sensory Processes

Vision reception involves light energies (the visible range of wavelengths in the electromagnetic spectrum) that enter the eye by passing through the cornea, pupil, and lens. They are detected by visual receptors in the retina. There they pass through neuronal tissue, are transduced into action potentials, and are transmitted via the **occipital nerve** to the visual region of the brain, where they are registered and interpreted as sights. The image is brought to the retina in an upside-down position but is transformed to an upright position by the brain. **Feature detector** neurons in the visual cortex are specialized and so are activated only by stimuli of a specific shape or pattern.

The **retina** is the light-sensitive surface at the back of the eyeball that has two kinds of receptors. **Cones** function primarily in daylight or high illumination. They are concentrated in the center of the eye, particularly in the **fovea**, an area of maximum visual acuity. **Rods** are receptors that function in dim light and are largely insensitive to color and fine detail. More numerous than cones, they are found throughout the retina, except in the center of the fovea.

 **Note!**

Two competing theories explain why not all cones receive all colors.

- **Trichromatic theory** states that cones differ in their color sensitivity.
- **Opponent-process channels theory** states that particular cones can receive signals of only one of two colors (e.g., red or green) at one time.

Dark adaptation is an increased sensitivity to light after being in a place of relative dimness. It results from changes in the chemical composition of the rods and cones during that time.

The **blind spot** is a place in each retina with no receptors. It is an opening where the optic nerve exits to the brain. It often is unnoticed because of past visual learning.

There are three different **properties of light** stimuli. **Color**, or **hue**, is determined by the wavelength of the light. The range of hues perceived by humans (from reds to blues) is the **visible spectrum**. A **pure spectral color** results from stimulation by only a narrow band of wavelengths. **Intensity** is the amount of physical energy produced by the light. This is perceived as **brightness**. Finally, **saturation** is due to the variety of wavelengths produced. A pure spectral color is completely saturated, whereas a light with many wavelengths is low in saturation, or "washed out."

Visual dysfunctions include total blindness, usually from damage to nerve tissue. Nearsightedness, farsightedness, and astigmatism result from light stimuli that are not focused properly on the retina. Color blindness occurs when particular cones are missing or malfunctioning.

✷ Did You Know?

The most common color blindness is an inability to recognize reds and greens. For this reason there are universal standards for traffic signals: red is always above green so that the position of the illuminated globe indicates whether the "on" light is red or green.

Hearing (or **audition**) is the reception of sound wave mechanical energy generated when a source vibrates, resulting in compression and expansion of adjacent molecules. This is carried to the hearing receptors, usually through air molecules.

The parts of the body involved in normal hearing are the outer ear, the middle ear, and the inner ear. The **outer ear** (or **pinna**) "traps" and funnels sound waves to the eardrum. The **middle ear** contains three small bones or **ossicles**, the **malleus, incus,** and **stapes** (also called the **hammer, anvil,** and **stirrup**), which transfer the vibrations to a second membrane, called the **oval window**. The **inner ear** contains the **cochlea**, a snaillike structure filled with fluid and hairlike receptors (**hair cells**) that transduce the mechanical energy into an action potential. From the cochlea, the signals are transmitted through the auditory nerve to the **auditory cortex** of the brain, where registration of sound takes place.

One property of sound waves is **frequency**, or the number of sound waves per second. This determines the **pitch** a listener hears (higher frequency equals higher pitch). **Amplitude** is the amount of energy in each wave and is measured by its height. This is reported in decibel units and is perceived as loudness. **Complexity** refers to the numbers of different sound waves that occur simultaneously and that determine the **timbre** or sound quality.

Identifying the direction of a sound source is called **auditory localization**. This depends on the discrepancy between the time one ear receives the sound and the time the other ear receives it.

Example 5.3 Sit with your eyes closed and have someone make a noise directly in front or back of you. Try to pinpoint the location of the sound. You may find that you are unable to determine the location because the auditory stimulus arrives at both ears simultaneously.

Damage to the conductive mechanisms (**conduction deafness**) or the nerves involved (**nerve deafness**) in hearing account for mild and partial **auditory dysfunctions**.

Smell (**olfaction**) and **taste** (**gustation**) are **chemical senses** that receive stimulus energy from chemical substances. Like the other senses, the signals are transduced into action potentials relayed to specialized areas of the brain to be recorded as odors or tastes.

Smell receptors are hair cells in the membranes of each nasal passage (**olfactory epithelium**). Taste receptors are specialized cells in the tongue; they have hairlike endings grouped together in **taste buds**. Taste receptors are sensitive to **sweet**, **sour**, **salty**, and **bitter**, with each type most sensitive to only one of these stimuli. **Flavor** results from the combination of taste and smell.

Dysfunctions of these senses are usually mild, unless there is nerve tissue damage. Permanent difficulties such as **anosmia**, the inability to smell normally, may result from a head injury or long-term asthma.

The skin (**cutaneous**) senses provide sensory experiences from **warm**, **cold**, **pressure**, and **pain** receptors in and under the skin. Certain areas, such as the face and hands, have many more receptors than do other areas, such as the back.

The stimuli received may be provided by either mechanical or radiant energy. Modification of the signals received, particularly those of pain, can occur. The **gate-control theory of pain** suggests that there are receptors that can send signals that make an individual more or less sensitive to pain.

Kinesthetic receptors are located in muscles, joints, tendons, and the skin. They provide information about changes in the activity and position of the body (**kinesthesis**) that aid in coordination. Which receptors are activated depends on the direction and angle of movement. The signals from the kinesthetic receptors are registered and interpreted in the brain. Dysfunctions occur when nervous system damage prevents signals from the receptors from registering.

Balance (the **vestibular** sense) has receptors in the inner ear. These consist of three semicircular canals and the vestibular sacs that contain hair cells that respond to changes in body orientation. Fluid in the **semicircular canals** moves with body rotation and generates displacement of the receptors. The hair cells of the **vestibular sacs** respond to the body's position or angle. Dysfunctions of balance may lead to vertigo or nystagmus (involuntary oscillation of the eyeballs).

Perception: External Cues

Perception is the process by which a person **interprets** sensory stimuli. It depends heavily on experience. Even assuming normal development, only a small portion of the information received will be processed and interpreted, a process known as **selection attention**.

External (stimulus) **cues** develop from the properties of stimuli. Interest in the effects of external stimuli on attention and perceptual development arose during the years of Gestalt psychology.

The **figure-ground relationship** determines how distinct the main stimulus (figure) is within the context (ground). The greater the **intensity** of a stimulus, the more likely it is that a subject will attend to it. **Contrast**, difference from the ground, also increases attention. Figure-ground relationships can be **unstable** if the figure can be perceived as the ground and vice versa. Figures may also be **ambiguous** if they can be interpreted in multiple ways.

Similarity of multiple stimuli, their **proximity**, and their **continuity** (flow) can affect how one attends to and understands them. People also provide **closure** to a stimulus by filling in gaps in incomplete information. Gestaltists also believed that given a choice of interpretations of a stimulus, people prefer **simplicity** to **complexity**.

Perceptual constancy refers to the phenomenon in which a stimulus is perceived to be unchanging in size, shape, brightness, and color although the stimulus itself does change. (For example, as you move away from a dinner plate on a table, the image on your retinas becomes more like an oval than a circle.)

Binocular depth cues depend on **retinal disparity**, the slight difference in the visual images on the retinas of the two eyes. The brain "blends" these images so one sees only one image with information about depth. The muscular movement involved in focusing an image on the retinas as one draws closer to an object is called **convergence**.

Monocular depth cues provide depth information using only one eye. They are **interposition, perspective, texture gradient**, and **shadow**.

Let's Compare ... ✔

- **Interposition**—An object blocks an object behind it.
- **Perspective**—Convergence of lines in distance.
- **Texture gradient**—Smoother textures in distance.
- **Shadow**—indicates distance, height, shape.

Perception: Internal Cues

Internal cues that affect perception appear to be a function of top-down and bottom-up processing. Previous learning, context, and expectations are among the factors that play a role in **top-down processing**. These influence closure, the interpretation of an ambiguous stimulus, selective attention, and the patterning or organization of information.

Bottom-up processing is recognition and processing of information about the individual components of stimuli. Both types of processing occur simultaneously and enable a person to respond appropriately.

Example 5.4 As you read this text, your perception of individual letters is based on bottom-up processing. Your understanding of the information is based on top-down processing influences, including your prior learning and the context in which you are reading.

Unusual Perceptual Experiences

An **illusion** is a stimulus that is interpreted incorrectly.

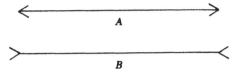

Figure 5-1 The Mueller-Lyer illusion.

Example 5.5 The famous Mueller-Lyer illusion (see Figure 5-1) shows how stimulus cues may lead to perceptual misunderstanding. Lines A and B are exactly the same length, but A appears shorter than B.

Subliminal perception is perception without awareness (below the absolute threshold). This is a research area fraught with difficulties because of individual differences in the absolute threshold and people's strong expectations about subliminal perceptions.

Even more suspect is research on **extrasensory perception (ESP)**. **Telepathy**, **precognition**, **clairvoyance**, and **psychokinesis** are ESP phenomena that have not been reliably demonstrated to exist.

Solved Problems

Solved Problem 5.1 Are sensations recognized when a receptor is activated? Is the process the same for each type of sensation?

Activation of a specialized nerve receptor begins the sensory process. The signal must be transduced into an action potential, transmitted through the sensory peripheral nervous system to the central nervous system, and "recorded" in the brain before the recognition of a sensation takes place.

This sequence—stimulus, receptor, sensory peripheral nerve, and central nervous system—is essentially the same for all sensory processes. Differences exist in the types of stimuli that activate the receptors, which parts of the sensory peripheral nervous system are at work, and which specialized parts of the cortex are activated.

Solved Problem 5.2 Describe how the process of seeing is similar to the process by which a camera works.

A camera is a container with an opening on one side and film on the opposite side. The eye is somewhat similar. The pupil of the eye serves as the opening, which can adjust to the amount of light being received. Directly behind this is the lens, which focuses the stimuli being received on the retina. The retina is similar to the film, located at the back of the eyeball and receiving the stimuli. Carrying the analogy further, the visual area of the brain is the processor, "developing" the signals transmitted from the retina.

Solved Problem 5.3 Why does a person feel dizzy after spinning?

Movement of the fluid in one or more of the semicircular canals in the ears does not end immediately when the body stops moving. It continues to "slosh around," and signals sent from the affected hair cells are interpreted as dizziness.

Chapter 6
CONSCIOUSNESS

IN THIS CHAPTER:

Characteristics of Consciousness

Consciousness is the term for internal mental experiences of which a person is aware. Many types of consciousness may be experienced, including thoughts, feelings, attention, memories, control of one's behavior, and dreams. Consciousness is a function of brain activity.

Differing **levels of consciousness** exist. Information at the **preconscious** level could reach conscious consideration easily but is not continuously in awareness. Automatic behaviors, such as driving a car and throwing a ball are examples. Information stored at the **unconscious** (or

subconscious) level often cannot be recalled or require considerable effort to access.

Example 6.1 Freud suggested that information at the unconscious level may be there because it is upsetting and has been purposely repressed. This idea is controversial and difficult to study experimentally.

Psychologists also distinguish between types of conscious processes. Some tasks require **controlled processing**, in which full concentration is necessary. Other tasks are completed without full awareness, operating with what has been called **automatic processing**. Many tasks advance from controlled to automatic processing as familiarity with a task increases.

Example 6.2 Initial attempts to use a computer keyboard require great concentration to learn the location of letters and numbers. As one develops familiarity with the task, the "typing" becomes automatic, allowing for other mental processes to occur simultaneously.

Techniques such as **electroencephalography (EEG), magnetic resonance imaging (MRI), computerized axial tomography (CAT) scans**, and **positron emission tomography (PET) scans** enable psychologists and neuroscientists to monitor and record activity in certain parts of the brain.

 **Note!**

The activity of the brain is similar when recalling actual events and recalling dreams, even though dreams include illogical and dramatic experiences that differ from waking-state experiences.

Limitations of consciousness have been documented. First, if brain processes are disrupted or destroyed, the conscious process may be upset or eliminated. Therefore, consciousness depends on the appropriate operation of the brain. Second, consciousness is limited to the person's capacity to receive and process information. In general, a person can concentrate on only one thought at a time. Third, environmental conditions such as interruptions, sensory deprivation or overload, fatigue, and drugs may alter conscious processes. Finally, behaviors such as meditation and drugs such as LSD seem to affect consciousness. Conditions outside the normal range are referred to as **altered states of consciousness**.

Altered States of Consciousness: Internal Influences

Internal influences on consciousness may be the result of past learning or internal body states. Some of the most widely studied conscious processes are those that occur during **sleep**.

Humans have a biological clock that operates in a rhythmic fashion and develops as a child becomes accustomed to environmental circumstances, resulting in daily rhythms (**circadian rhythms**) of behavior such as hunger, hormonal flow, and sleep. These usually match a 24-hour day, although a person in an environment where time cues are completely eliminated may establish a different rhythm.

 Did You Know?

Jet lag results from disruption of circadian rhythms, not just from lack of sleep.

Sleep shows rhythmic patterns within the sleeping period. Research done with subjects willing to sleep in laboratory situations has identified four different depths or **stages of sleep** by recording changes in EEG waves. A person is likely to move through this 90-minute cycle several times during one night. It is marked by a slowing of brain wave activity and reduced responsiveness to outside stimuli.

Stage 1 sleep is preceded by **alpha** brain waves (approximately 10 cycles per second), which are replaced by slower, more irregular **theta** waves. The period just before sleep actually begins is referred to as a **hypnagogic** state. Stage 2 includes continued theta activity, with occasional **spindles** (bursts of 14-cycle-per-second activity), while in stage 3, **delta** waves (2 cycles per second) are added. Finally, stage 4 shows almost exclusive delta wave activity.

A period of heightened brain activity, cerebral blood flow, and **rapid eye movement (REM)** occurs after each 90 minute cycle. REM sleep is associated with dreaming. It gets longer after each successive sleep cycle, lasting 30 to 60 minutes by the end of the night. REM sleep is known as **paradoxical sleep** because heart rate, respiration rate, and EEG patterns closely resemble those during an awake state. However, activity of the cranial and spinal motor neurons is inhibited during REM, leading to a loss of muscle tone and diminished chance of movement.

There are several explanations for why people dream, although there is little agreement. Some research suggests that dreams serve a recuperative function. Irritability, anxiety, and even hallucinations may result from a lack of REM sleep. People deprived of REM sleep later show a rebound of REM sleep, incorporating more of it than usual. Freud suggested that dreams represent unconscious wish fulfillment and that dreams might threaten conscious awareness. He distinguished between the **manifest** and **latent content** (symbolic meaning) of dreams. Dream analysis was thought to be an important source of psychotherapeutic information. Other explanations of dreaming focus on the need to dream as a means of dealing with daily concerns.

Sleep itself appears to serve a **restorative function**. Sleep deprivation can produce fatigue, perceptual distortion, diminished cerebral functioning, and disruption of bodily processes.

Not all people experience smooth patterns of sleep. **Insomnia**, the inability to fall asleep or continue sleeping, is the most common sleep disorder. **Sleep apnea** involves a complete stoppage of breathing. Associated with obesity and alcohol use in adults, it is also thought to be a possible cause of **sudden infant death syndrome (SIDS).** Sudden, uncontrollable attacks of 15 to 20 minute sleep during normal waking mark **narcolepsy. Somnambulism (sleepwalking)** typically occurs during non-REM sleep. Most incidents occur in children who do not recall the incidents upon awakening.

Meditation techniques are used to try to "focus" conscious processes. **Concentrative meditation** limits conscious attention to a specific object or sound. A state of emptiness accompanied by clarity of thought is the goal. **Opening-up meditation** is an attempt to develop constant attention to everything that occurs. The goal is to produce a broad understanding of the total environment. Both techniques produce changed states of consciousness for some practitioners. Many claim benefits, including increased understanding of the self. Sometimes meditation is accompanied by changes in physiological processes.

In **biofeedback** a person observes measurements of bodily processes that are otherwise unobservable. The person then learns to regulate processes, such as heart rate or blood pressure, that usually are thought to be involuntary. This is accomplished by using a monitoring device that indicates the status of the otherwise "hidden" variable. As the person learns to control the process, this is reflected by a change in the signal. The feedback provides information that helps the person focus conscious processes in order to manipulate bodily activity.

Example 6.3 Migraine headaches may result from excessive blood flow in the brain. To overcome this, biofeedback techniques have been used to teach a person to adjust blood flow so that more blood goes to other parts of the body, thus decreasing the headache symptoms.

Altered States of Consciousness: External Influences

External stimuli influence an individual's consciousness. **Psychoactive drugs**, such as depressants, stimulants, narcotics, and hallucinogens, affect the central nervous system (CNS), causing subjective changes in perception, emotion, and other conscious processes. The study of the psychological effect of drugs is called **psychopharmacology.**

Drug use may not result in impairment, but with **drug abuse**, users may be significantly impaired. **Physiological drug dependence** occurs when the use of a drug causes a change in the body's chemical balance and only continued use can maintain that changed status. **Psychological drug dependence** is the belief or feeling that the drug is needed.

As the body becomes accustomed to the use of a drug, it often develops a **drug tolerance**, in which the effect produced can be achieved only if a greater amount is used. Stopping the use of drugs can lead to **withdrawal effects**, or unpleasant side effects produced by the body's compensatory or tolerance mechanisms.

 **Note!**

Some forms of drug abuse may not be recognized. Many people abuse caffeine, drinking coffee to the extent that failure to have it causes various forms of impairment.

Depressants ("downers") slow the operation of the CNS. **Alcohol** is one of the most widely used psychoactive drugs that can depress CNS functioning. The mental "high" produced by alcohol is accompanied by lowered inhibitions and impairment of motor coordination. Extreme use can cause death. **Barbiturates** are depressants that are commonly prescribed to treat insomnia or relieve stress. Nembutal and Seconal are often used.

Narcotics relieve anxiety, produce relaxation, or reduce pain. Abuse of the two most common, **heroin** and **morphine**, is widespread. Repeated use leads to an increasing physiological dependence. This results in tolerance and withdrawal symptoms.

Stimulants elevate heart rate, blood pressure, and muscle tension. **Caffeine** is present in many products. The **nicotine** in tobacco products activates neurons in much the same manner as does cocaine; both are highly addictive. **Cocaine** creates feelings of euphoria, confidence, and alertness. The fast-acting version is "crack," which is smoked and so enters the bloodstream and affects the brain within seconds. Prolonged use of cocaine or crack may lead to psychotic behavior. **Amphetamines**

("speed") include Benzedrine and Dexedrine. The use of these in relatively small amounts produces increased alertness, energy, and positive feelings. When used excessively, amphetamines can produce feelings of persecution, negative emotions, and even death.

Many classify **marijuana** as a **hallucinogenic drug**. Using it may produce elation and a perceived enrichment of sensory experiences. The effects may be a function not only of the drug itself but also of the expectations of the user. Some studies have suggested a **reverse tolerance effect** in which of the less of the drug is needed to produce the same high. Other hallucinogens, such as **LSD**, **PCP**, and **mescaline**, typically produce strong hallucinations and unpredictable effects.

Hypnosis involves external control of consciousness and is marked by increased suggestibility. A hypnotized person may experience a distorted perception of reality, and show relaxation or alertness, depending on the hypnotist's instructions. Some psychologists believe that reports of hypnotic states are "faked behaviors" that represent the subject's desire to please the hypnotist.

> The EEG measurements of a hypnotized person are comparable to those of an awake person rather than those of a sleeping person.

Consciousness may be affected by **brain damage**, although it is not possible to predict all the effects that may be produced by brain damage. Changes in emotional reactions, memory skills, or perception have been demonstrated by testing patients before and after surgery.

Solved Problems

Solved Problem 6.1 Social learning is a major influence on internal control of consciousness. What kinds of effects might be expected?

Social learning may facilitate or inhibit conscious processes. For example, if a botanist and a geologist hiked through a forest together, each would likely have a different consciousness of the experience.

Solved Problem 6.2 Are drug abuse and drug dependence the same?

Abuse is misuse of a drug but it does not necessarily indicate physiological or psychological dependence. For example, a person who is not an alcoholic may drink enough to pass out at a party. This is abuse of alcohol, but is not necessarily an indication of dependence.

Chapter 7
LEARNING

Learning is a relatively permanent change in behavior as a result of experience. Learning and performance are not necessarily the same. Observable behavior (**performance**) does not always reveal what an organism has learned.

Classical Conditioning

Classical conditioning occurs when an organism learns to respond in a particular way to a stimulus that previously did not produce that response. The once "neutral" stimulus becomes response-producing because it is paired (or associated) with another stimulus that does produce the response. A behaviorist explanation emphasizes **contiguity**, the "external" arrangement of the occurrence of the two stimuli in a relatively close time frame. By contrast, a cognitive explanation stresses the "internal" perceived **contingency** in which the originally neutral stimulus comes to predict the onset of the other response-producing stimulus. Classical conditioning also has been called **respondent conditioning** or **Pavlovian**

conditioning. The term "respondent" implies that the learned response is elicited involuntarily from the subject rather than being produced in a voluntary (or operant) manner.

 Don't Get Confused!

Just as you may have a different explanation from a friend for the same event, psychologists can also disagree about explanations for events. Behavioral psychologists emphasize external circumstances. Cognitive psychologists emphasize internal ones.

A stimulus that is originally neutral and comes to be response-producing is a **conditioned stimulus (CS)**. A stimulus that produces the response on the first trial and every one thereafter is called an **unconditioned stimulus (US)**. The response elicited by a US is called an **unconditioned response (UR)**. Eventually the same type of response will occur at the presentation of the CS; this response is called the **conditioned response (CR)**. An **orienting response (OR)** often occurs for the first few trials as the subject initially responds by determining where the stimulus originated or what the stimulus is.

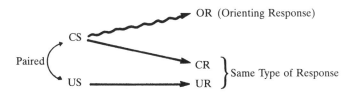

Figure 7-1 An illustration of the classical conditioning paradigm.

Example 7.1 Ivan Pavlov (1849–1936) used dogs in his original studies. He found that presentations of meat powder (US) caused the dogs to salivate (UR). Pavlov then paired a ringing bell (CS) with the presentation of the meat powder. This soon led the dogs to salivate (CR) at the sound of the bell. The OR occurred in the first few trials when the dogs turned their heads to determine the origin of the bell.

The paired CS and US may occur exactly together, or there may be a time interval between them. The time between their onset is the **interstimulus interval (ISI)**. Contiguity describes the timing relationship between the CS and the US, while contingency refers to the perceived cognitive connection between them. In general, CRs are most likely to develop in ISI situations where the CS precedes the US. Usually the timing is brief (seconds or fractions of seconds) for successful conditioning, although some examples exist to the contrary.

Example 7.2 The Pavlovian experiment may be conducted with several different ISI arrangements for the bell (CS) and the meat powder (US).

Simultaneous conditioning: They are presented at the same time.
Delayed conditioning: The bell comes on first and stays on until the meat powder is presented.
Trace conditioning: The bell comes on and goes off before the meat powder is presented.
Backward conditioning: The meat powder is presented before the bell is rung.
Temporal conditioning: The bell is never rung. The CS is a constant time period, such as 5 minutes. The meat powder is presented every 5 minutes.

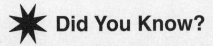 **Did You Know?**

Learned taste aversions are examples of classical conditioning when the ISI is many hours. Ingestion of a food that is followed by illness some time later will often lead to a learned aversion to the food.

Extinction is the presentation of the CS alone, without the US, for repeated trials so that the CR returns to its original (preconditioning) level. Resistance to extinction is one measure of the strength of a CR. Assuming that the US can be treated as a **reinforcer** (an event that strengthens or maintains the response), resistance to extinction can be increased by using **partial reinforcement**. This occurs when the CS is paired with the US in some but not all trials. It is described in percentages; for example, if the CS is paired with the US in half the trials, reinforcement is 50 percent. A CR acquired under partial reinforcement takes longer to learn but, once acquired, is more resistant to extinction than a CR established under continuous (100 percent) reinforcement. This is the **partial reinforcement effect (PRE)**.

If, after extinction, the CS is presented without the US, the CR sometimes will reappear. This is called **spontaneous recovery**.

Stimulus generalization is demonstrated when a CR is made not only to the original CS but also to other stimuli that are similar to that CS. If this is based on the properties of the stimulus, it is called **primary stimulus generalization**. Humans, who have a command of language and other symbols, show an additional form of generalization called **secondary stimulus generalization**. A human's CR may be given to other stimuli that are similar in meaning to the original CS.

A subject who gives the CR to a particular CS but not to similar stimuli shows **discrimination** among the stimuli.

Example 7.3 Pavlov's dogs would have shown complete stimulus generalization if they had salivated in response to any noise. If they had responded to the bell but not to other similar sounds, they would have shown complete discrimination. Pavlov showed that when dogs were forced to discriminate between two very similar stimuli, they sometimes showed distress. Pavlov called this **experimental neurosis**.

When the strength of the CR is near its maximum value, the CS that elicits the CR may take on the role of a US, so that a new pairing can be established in which a new CS is paired with the well-established CS. Repeated presentation leads to the elicitation of the same type of CR by presentation of the new CS alone. This is **higher-order conditioning**.

The principles of classical conditioning can be applied to other psychological phenomena. When a previously neutral stimulus (CS) is paired with a reinforcer (US) and the CS takes on reinforcing properties, a **secondary (conditioned) reinforcer** is established. Frequently, secondary reinforcers are verbal stimuli that become meaningful as reinforcers only after pairings of this sort. This principle applies in establishing **conditioned aversive stimuli**.

Phobias are intense fears established in the same manner as other CRs. A previously neutral stimulus (CS) is paired with a fear-producing stimulus (US), and the CS takes on fear-producing attributes. Similar to establishing secondary reinforcers, this is an illustration of **secondary** or **conditioned emotion**.

Example 7.4 Two-year-old Bailey tries to eat a bug. Her father stops her and, while doing so, says, "Oh, don't eat that . . . it's pooky!" Bailey sees dad make an unpleasant face. Several additional pairings of "pooky" with similar unpleasant expressions are all it takes for Bailey to understand that "pooky" means something is bad. This is a conditioned aversive stimulus.

Example 7.5 Imagine stepping into an elevator that plunged 20 floors before the emergency brake saved you from crashing. It is probably easy to understand that your next confrontation with an elevator might be highly fear-producing. The previously neutral elevator stimulus takes on fear-producing qualities from the single CS-US pairing.

Operant Conditioning

Operant conditioning is learning that involves changing the probability of a response by manipulating the consequences of that response. The underlying principle is the **law of effect**, proposed by E. L. Thorndike (1874–1949). The law of effect states that responses followed by positive consequences are more likely to be repeated than responses followed by negative consequences. Thorndike believed that the law of effect was "automatic," that the organism did not have to understand the link between the response and the result. Operant conditioning is also called **instrumental conditioning** or **Skinnerian conditioning** for B. F. Skinner (1904–1990), a leading investigator of the principles of operant conditioning. The term **instrumental** is used because the response is thought to be helpful in achieving a desired goal. The **operant response** is a voluntary response made by an organism. Operant responses may be learned in sequence (a **chain** of behavior).

Typically, the goal achieved in instrumental conditioning is referred to as a **reinforcement**. **Positive reinforcement** means that the presence of a particular stimulus strengthens or maintains a response. **Negative reinforcement** means that the removal or absence of an aversive stimulus strengthens or maintains the response.

When a less probable or less desired response is encouraged by the promise of the opportunity to perform a more desired response, the more desired response serves as a reinforcer. This is called the **Premack principle** after David Premack, who first studied this.

Occasionally, misinterpretations of a circumstance occur when a reinforcer happens to follow a response by chance (a **noncontingent reinforcer**). Organisms sometimes appear to demonstrate a link between the response that preceded the reinforcer and the outcome of reinforcement, a result that may lead to **superstitious behavior**.

The most common measure of the acquisition of an operant response is a **cumulative record** of the response. This indicates the number of satisfactory responses made in a given time period.

A device often used in operant conditioning research is an **operant conditioning chamber** (or a **Skinner box**), shown in Figure 7-2.

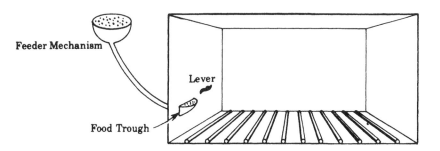

Figure 7-2 A Skinner box.

Example 7.6 An untrained and hungry laboratory rat placed in a Skinner box eventually may learn to press the lever, which will activate the feeder mechanism and deliver food pellets into the trough. This is a positive reinforcement situation. If the grid floor were electrified so that a mild electric shock served as an aversive stimulus, the rat could learn to press the lever to turn off the shock. This is negative reinforcement.

To encourage the acquisition of the operant response, the process of **shaping**—the reinforcement of closer and closer approximations to the desired response—sometimes is used.

Example 7.7 When an untrained rat is placed in a Skinner box, it is possible to speed the acquisition of the lever-pressing response by using a shaping procedure. With a remote control, the experimenter can reinforce the rat's approaches to the lever, any indications of interest in the lever, placing a paw on the lever, and finally pressing the lever—a sequence of responses that leads to the appropriate response.

When aversive stimuli are involved, acquisition is categorized in several ways. If the response made terminates an already present aversive stimulus, it is an **escape response**. An **avoidance response** means that an organism responds in a way that keeps an aversive stimulus from being delivered. **Punishment** occurs when a response is followed by an aversive stimulus. **Noncontingent punishment** may result in superstitious behavior.

 Don't Be Confused!

Reinforcement increases the probability of a response. Punishment decreases the probability of a response. Negative reinforcement and punishment are two different consequences with opposite effects.

Extinction is accomplished by terminating the delivery of reinforcement. The result is a decreased rate of responding until it reaches the preconditioning level. The effect of **partial reinforcement** in operant conditioning is the same as in classical conditioning; acquisition of the response under partial reinforcement leads to greater resistance to extinction than does continuous reinforcement.

The effects of partial reinforcement have been investigated by arranging the contingencies according to several principles or **schedules of reinforcement**. The four basic formats are:

Fixed ratio (FR): Reinforcement is contingent on a certain number of responses that remain constant throughout the procedure.

Fixed interval (FI): Reinforcement is contingent on a correct response being made at the end of a specified time interval that does not vary.

Variable ratio (VR): Reinforcement is contingent on responding, but the number of responses required varies, usually randomly, from trial to trial.

Variable interval (VI): Reinforcement is contingent on responding at the end of a period of time, but the time period changes, usually randomly.

Each of the schedules usually produces a particular pattern of responding, described below and illustrated in Figure 7-3:

FR: Bursts of responses closely matching the required number of responses are followed by brief pauses just after the reinforcement.

FI: There is no or very slow responding during the early part of the interval, which then gives way to a high rate of responding just as the interval nears completion.

VR: A constant high rate of responding develops as the subject learns that more responses mean more reinforcements. However, the subject cannot determine how many responses must be made for each reinforcement.

VI: A slow, steady rate of responding occurs. The rate is not important, but a correct response must be made at the end of each time period. The subject guards against missing the end of an interval by continuing to deliver steady performance.

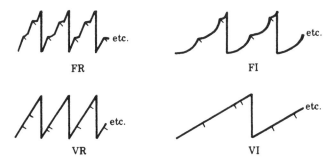

Figure 7-3 Cumulative response records for different schedules of reinforcement. Each "hash mark" is the delivery of reinforcement. Time is plotted on the x-axis; frequency of responding is on the y-axis.

Combinations of the basic schedules lead to more complex ones. A **multiple schedule** requires the subject to satisfy two or more independent schedules that are presented successively. A **compound schedule** reinforces a single response according to the requirements of two or more schedules operating simultaneously. A **concurrent schedule** reinforces the subject when two or more responses are made to satisfy the requirements of two or more schedules at the same time.

Example 7.8 Using profanity may be considered appropriate when talking with a peer, less appropriate with parents, and inappropriate with a religious leader. The different conversational partners serve as the cue stimuli for what is multiple schedules of reinforcement.

Discriminative stimuli (cues) indicate when responding is appropriate or inappropriate. These are not considered conditioned stimuli because they do not elicit specific responses, but they do serve as signals for responses.

Stimulus generalization is when the subject responds not only to the original (discriminative) stimulus but to other, similar stimuli. **Stimulus discrimination** occurs when the subject distinguishes between the original discriminative stimulus and other similar stimuli, making the operant response in the presence of the original, but not other stimuli. In operant situations, psychologists sometimes refer to **response generalization** as having occurred. They do this because there is not a specific response that is required to perform most operant tasks, but rather a "family" of responses.

There are many possible applications of operant conditioning in family life, education, business, and animal training, for example.

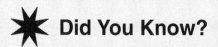

Did You Know?

Behavior modification techniques used in therapeutic settings rely on operant conditioning.

Cognitive Social Learning

Cognitive learning refers to acquisition using mental or cognitive processes. Very often, this occurs after observing others' behaviors. Thus, many psychologists refer to this as **cognitive social learning** or **observational learning**; other labels include **modeling**, **learning by imitation**, and **social learning**. Although there is some evidence that cognitive learning occurs in other species, most research has been conducted with humans. In general, what seems to be learned is an abstract representation (a **schema**) of the behavior observed, but there are occasional examples of **pure imitation** of another's behavior.

Two considerations are relevant to understanding cognitive learning. First, external reinforcement facilitates cognitive learning, but the response can be learned because it has been observed, not because it has been reinforced. Second, many activities provoke a sense of **intrinsic** (or internal) reinforcement.

Vicarious learning occurs when an observer notes not only the response of another, but also the consequences of that response for the other. The schema (or expectation) that develops includes both the pattern of responding and the knowledge of what the consequence of making that response might be.

Example 7.9 You may have experienced vicarious learning if you have observed someone suffer a burn. Suppose you watched your sister lean against an electric range just after one of the burners was turned off. You saw the burn she received and her pain. You did not have to lean on the hot burner yourself to know that it could hurt you.

Much cognitive learning depends on verbal representations of a behavior rather than observation of an actual behavior. This ability distinguishes humans from other species. **Symbolic learning** reduces the time and effort necessary for learning many behaviors.

Observers are selective in their choice of models. This is based on the **status** of the potential model, including characteristics such as the position the model holds and the power or influence the model has.

Solved Problems

Solved Problem 7.1 Playing in the backyard one day, 3-year-old Kyle is on a swing when a rabbit suddenly appears and startles her. She slips off the swing, hurts her arm, and cries with pain. Later, after calming down, Kyle returns to the backyard. While she is standing on the grass, another rabbit hops into view and Kyle begins to cry. Identify the US, UR, CS, and CR.

The US is the pain. It generates the UR of crying. The CS is the rabbit. Presumably, the rabbit's appearance was originally a neutral stimulus; however, it came to be paired with the pain and later produced the CR of crying at the sight of the rabbit.

Solved Problem 7.2 A student attending a class where an instructor gives unannounced ("pop") quizzes probably should study according to one of the basic schedules of reinforcement. Which one?

Pop quizzes may occur at any time. Therefore, the student needs to be ready for one at any class meeting and should study a little bit every day. This is a variable interval schedule, where the payoff comes after a certain amount of time but the time periods are not always the same.

Solved Problem 7.3 Subjects were shown a video of aggressive behavior that is ordinarily disapproved of. However, the aggressive behavior shown on the tape went unpunished. The subjects were as likely to imitate the aggression as were subjects shown a video that depicted the same behaviors being rewarded. What term describes this and what explanation accounts for it?

The subjects were experiencing vicarious reinforcement. They saw the positive consequences of normally disapproved responses. In the second video, the responses yielded direct positive reinforcement, while in the first, the absence of anticipated punishment indicated permissiveness and reduced fears that might normally accompany such behavior. This fear reduction served as negative reinforcement, with the removal of the aversive stimulus (fear) strengthening the likelihood of copying the observed aggression.

Chapter 8
RETENTION AND FORGETTING

IN THIS CHAPTER:

- ✔ *Definitions*
- ✔ *Types of Storage*
- ✔ *Measures of Retention*
- ✔ *Theories of Forgetting*
- ✔ *Ways to Improve Memory*
- ✔ *Special Issues in Retention*
- ✔ *Solved Problems*

Definitions

Retention is the storage of learning over a period of time called the **retention interval**. Memory includes both retention and **retrieval**. **Forgetting** is a loss of retention or an inability to retrieve. Retention is often evaluated using the **information-processing approach**. Psychologists interested in representing learning in terms of computers have analyzed learning as an **input-processing-output sequence**.

Types of Storage

Information in **sensory storage** is held in an unprocessed form before being "read out," categorized, or interpreted. This kind of storage lasts for a very brief period. Two forms of sensory storage have been studied: **echoic** storage of auditory signals and **iconic** storage of visual signals. Materials are processed from sensory storage into short-term or long-term storage, or they are lost.

Short-term storage extends from 1 to 30 seconds after exposure to a stimulus item. Initial processing of the item takes place during this period, but if further processing does not take place, the item is lost. Short-term storage is also called **working memory**, implying that conscious activity is being devoted to the information. The amount of material that can be held in this active state is limited and depends on **chunking**. Some psychologists consider working memory to be a special part of long-term memory that moves currently activated information to and from short-term storage. The idea is that **parallel processing** may occur, so that disparate elements of information may be simultaneously active.

Example 8.1 Remembering a string of digits can be altered to be easier or harder. Consider 2-7-5-8-7-3-5-2-1-9-7-5. If you try to remember these digits in the order presented, you should remember at least the first five digits, usually will remember seven, and may remember nine. It is easy to expand the total number of digits remembered by chunking them into two-digit numbers, that is, as 27, 58, 73, 52, 19, and 75. Now there are only six units of information, less than what is typically thought to be the capacity of short-term storage (**7 plus or minus 2**) but the six units contain more total information than the digits treated individually.

Long-term storage occurs when materials in sensory or short-term storage are processed, rehearsed, or encoded over a period of longer than 30 seconds. It is thought to have unlimited capacity; items in long-term storage may also have unlimited retention intervals. How items enter long-term storage is debated. Psychologists suggest that a process of **consolidation**, the forming of a fixed or stable memory, must occur, involving activity of the central nervous system. Recent studies have focused on the activation of a protein in nerve cells that causes growth of dendrites and therefore strengthens the connections at synapses.

> # Think About It:
>
> The relation between dendrite growth and memory shows how the brain is related to behavior.

Psychologists make a distinction between **semantic** and **episodic memory**, with the former referring to storage based on the meaning of words and the latter identifying memory of a particular event. Differences also exist between declarative and procedural knowledge. **Declarative knowledge** refers to remembered facts, while **procedural knowledge** includes skills. In addition, some distinguish between explicit and implicit memory; **explicit memory** involves effort, while **implicit memory** is produced relatively effortlessly.

Example 8.2 Talking about cycling with someone else involves semantic memory ("The frame I have is made of space-age materials!") or episodic memory ("That day I was pushing hard to get to the top of that steep hill."). Declarative memory is illustrated by knowing facts about bicycles ("Many bikes have at least 21 gears."), while procedural knowledge is shown when actually riding a bike (the skill or motor performance). Recognizing landmarks and unconsciously turning while talking with a riding partner illustrate implicit memory. Actually naming the roads that made up the route involves a conscious effort to recall each one, evidence of explicit memory.

Measures of Retention

In **recognition** measures of retention, the subject is presented, with the correct answer, often as one of a number of available answers. The subject responds by selecting the answer thought to be correct. In **recall** measures, a minimum cue statement or question is presented, and the subject is required to supply additional information. In some situations, subjects may have to **relearn** materials they have learned before. The amount of

time or the number of trials required may be compared to the amount or number required for original learning. Measurement of retention can be computed in terms of the **savings score** shown in relearning: Savings score = (original learning—relearning) / original learning. By multiplying this value by 100, one arrives at a percentage that may be viewed as retention. Estimates of retention may vary, depending on the measure of retention used.

Example 8.3 A subject might learn the names of all the major league baseball teams. The subject might then learn the names of all the teams in the National Football League. Later, when retention for baseball teams is tested, a recognition test might yield a score of 65 percent, recall might be 40 percent, yet relearning might be −5 percent. The last result could occur because of confusion produced by the fact that many cities have one or more teams in both sports and also from names appearing in both sports but for different cities.

Psychologists represent acquisition and storage using graphs with performance plotted as a function of time or trials. These are called **learning curves**.

Example 8.4 Students learn keyboarding, or the ability to type using the letters and numbers on the keyboard of a computer. The performance measure used might be the number of words correctly typed in 2 minutes. This can be plotted against the amount of time spent practicing, as shown in Figure 8-1.

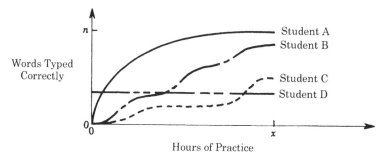

Figure 8-1 Sample learning curves for four students.

Occasionally, there is a period of no improvement, preceded and followed by periods of improvement in performance. This is a **plateau** in the learning curve. When a subject achieves maximum or nearly maximum performance, the learning curve levels off. This leveling of the curve is called an **asymptote**. The general pattern for loss of retention discovered by Hermann Ebbinghaus (1850–1909) over 100 years ago is that the greatest loss occurs soon after acquisition, with the rate of loss diminishing after that. This is known as the **curve of forgetting**. While the general form of the curve seems to hold for many cases, the exact level and shape may vary somewhat, depending on individual variables such as motivation and the materials learned. This is illustrated in the following example and in Figure 8-2.

Example 8.5 A group of subjects is asked to learn these items: "Horse, cow, giraffe, Oklahoma, mouse, dog, monkey, pig, cat, lamb, bird, snake, rat, bear." The **von Restorff effect** (or **isolation effect**) would be shown if subjects tended to learn and remember the one distinctive item—"Oklahoma"—better than most of the rest of the list. The subjects also would be likely to remember the first ("horse, cow") and last items ("rat, bear") quite well, illustrating the **serial position effect**.

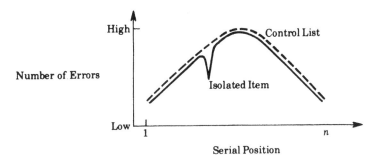

Figure 8-2 The serial position and von Restorff effects.

Theories of Forgetting

One theory suggests that forgetting results from **failure to retrieve** stored materials. Organization in storage, poor prompting, inappropriate motivation, or other variables might keep the person from retrieving the stored materials. Changes in the cue, suggestions for new ways to organize the material, and other alterations have shown that performance can improve considerably, lending support to this idea.

Another theory proposes that poor retention occurs because of disuse of learned materials, so that the memory trace fades and the memory eventually is lost. Practice will counteract this effect. The curve of forgetting provides support for this **fading of the memory trace theory**.

Forgetting could be due to **distortions of the memory trace**, as when some materials incorporated into memory are only partially accurate. The altered meanings of the stored materials make accurate recollection impossible.

Freud's psychoanalytic theory of **repression** suggests that some forgetting occurs because a person wishes to forget something to protect the self. Freud believed that such memories continued to influence behavior in the form of **unconscious motives**. Whereas experimental evidence supporting repression has not been produced, repression has been used in case histories to account for forgetting.

One of the best documented theories proposes that retention loss results from **interference** from other materials. This has been studied by investigating what effect one learning task has on the retention of other learning. The experimental design to test **proactive interference (PI)** is as follows:

	Step 1	Step 2		Step 3
Experimental group	Learn A	Learn B	Rest	Test B
Control group	Put in time	Learn B	Rest	Test B

If the control group does better than the experimental group on the test, it may be concluded that the task A materials interfered with the later retention of task B materials (PI).

Retroactive interference (**RI**) is tested similarly, using the following design:

	Step 1	Step 2		Step 3
Experimental group	Learn 1	Learn 2	Rest	Test 1
Control group	Learn 1	Put in time	Rest	Test 1

If the control group's performance on test 1 is better than the experimental group's performance, task 2 learning has interfered with the retention of task 1 (RI).

Ways to Improve Memory

Rehearsal (or repetition) is perhaps the most important way to influence acquisition. Rehearsal allows for the consolidation of information into long-term storage. Mere repetition is referred to as **maintenance rehearsal** or **shallow processing**. To ensure a greater likelihood that the information will be held in long-term storage, **elaborative rehearsal** or **deep processing** should be used.

Organization may be imposed either by the material itself or by the learner. Sensible organization usually leads to improved acquisition and retrieval, especially if the learner takes an active part in developing the organization.

Think About It:

- Files scattered around an office are more difficult to locate and retrieve than are organized files. The same is true for acquired information.
- Thinking about how a "filing" metaphor applies to memory is an example of elaborative rehearsal. Using such metaphors can suggest new ideas about memory.

Information that lends itself to creating **images** is more likely to be acquired and retained than is abstract information. Other memory-enhancing techniques, called **mnemonics**, include the **method of loci**, where information is cataloged as if in particular places; the **keyword technique**, which involves linking the information with specific prompts; and **rhyming**, where information is "forced" into a sound-alike format.

Overlearning is practice that occurs after a performance criterion has been reached. It is reported as a percentage of the time or number of trials needed for original learning. The law of diminishing returns operates for overlearning. While 50 percent overlearning usually results in significant improvement in acquisition and retention, 100 percent overlearning helps only a bit more.

Example 8.6 A subject took 16 trials to learn a list of nonsense syllables (consonant-vowel-consonant sequences such as YOF). If the subject continues to practice the correct order of the list for eight more trials, 50 percent overlearning will have occurred.

Transfer of training (or **transfer of learning**) occurs when learning one set of materials influences later learning of another set. The experimental design to test this is as follows:

	Step 1	Step 2
Experimental group	Learn task A	Learn task B
Control group	Put in time	Learn task B

To avoid possible biases because of warm-up or fatigue effects, the control group is kept busy doing an unrelated task during step 1, while the experimental group is learning task A. The test of transfer comes in step 2. If the experimental group learns and retains task B more easily than the control group, **positive transfer** has occurred. If the experimental group has more difficulty than the control group, **negative transfer** has occurred. If both groups learn task B equally well, **no transfer** (or **neutral transfer**) has occurred. A special case of transfer is **learning to learn**. A person may learn general principles and then use the general principles in later learning.

Example 8.7 Learning to play the piano would lead to positive transfer when learning to play the organ. However, learning to play the piano might hinder learning to play drums. Negative transfer might result because the manual skills developed in piano playing are so different from those required for drumming. Learning to play the piano would have no transfer effects for learning to speak Spanish.

 **Note!**

You can apply techniques such as elaborative rehearsal and the use of mnemonics to this material. Doing these things represents learning to learn.

Several **other practice variables** influence the acquisition and retention of materials. Included are **knowledge of results (KR)**, or feedback, the information about the effects of a response. In general, immediate KR is more beneficial than delayed KR, because the subject often treats KR as if it were reinforcement.

Another consideration is **distribution of practice** so that blocks of acquisition trials are interspersed with rest periods. This seems to improve acquisition and retention. When acquisition trials are massed together, performance suffers.

Example 8.8 A practical application of distribution of practice occurs in study sessions. Acquisition and retention of new materials seem to proceed more easily if studying is divided into study sessions and breaks.

Practice is more effective if it is done in an **active** rather than a **passive** manner. Active discussion of new materials is likely to promote acquisition and retention of those materials, while a more passive, reading-only approach is less likely to do so. Also, for some tasks, an initial period of **warm-up** is necessary before acquisition can take place.

A final consideration is called the **whole-part distinction**. Efforts may be focused on acquiring all the materials to be learned at one time (the whole method) or only segments of the materials (the part method). In the part method, the subject may divide the materials into several units, studying each separately and trying to bring them all together only after each has been mastered individually. The subject may also incorporate an "add-on" technique in which one unit is learned, a second is added to it, and so on. This is called the **progressive-part** method.

Special Issues in Retention

Several unusual aspects of retention are presented in this section to give a sense of the considerations psychologists must address.

Reduced memory functioning of several sorts have been grouped under the general heading **amnesia**. **Retrograde amnesia** is an inability to retrieve memories of events that occurred before a trauma that caused the memory loss. **Anterograde amnesia** refers to an inability to form memories for events that occur after the precipitating trauma. **Infantile amnesia** describes the common finding that memories for the first few years of life are typically nonexistent.

Context can influence acquisition and retention. The meaning of material may be inferred from the use of material in a particular setting. Also, associations between material and the context that promote acquisition and retention may result when material is presented in one setting and then tested later in the same setting. This is referred to as **state-dependent** or **context-dependent memory**.

The **tip-of-the-tongue phenomenon** describes a situation in which retrieval of information from long-term storage is not readily accomplished, but approximations of the answer are attempted. Similar sounds, the same number of syllables, or the same initial letter may be used in attempts to determine the correct response.

Eyewitness testimony about crimes provides information used in many legal settings. Research has shown that these reports are frequently inaccurate and subject to manipulation by the kinds of questions asked. Some witnesses make errors when asked to report what they observed because they are eager to help and so "manufacture" reports that seem appropriate for the situation. Furthermore, the witnesses are likely to believe the reports are true even when they contain combinations of truth and errors, as is usually the case. The reports of children are especially influenced by the questions asked by others.

Example 8.9 Laboratory evidence for the inaccuracy of eyewitness testimony includes a series of studies in which all subjects were exposed to the same stimuli but the questions asked of them were phrased in varying ways. For example, when asked how fast two cars were going when they "smashed" into each other, subjects estimated a speed almost 10 miles per hour faster than the speed estimated by subjects who were asked the speed when the cars "contacted" each other.

Solved Problems

Solved Problem 8.1 Suppose you are sitting in a totally darkened room. Someone else in the room waves a small flashlight in a figure-eight pattern. What do you see and why?

You are likely to "see" a tracery of light rather than a single moving point of light. Although the entire figure eight probably is not recorded at one time (unless the person is moving the light at a very rapid pace), at least part of the figure seems to be present. The explanation of this phenomenon is that you are holding sensory storage of the moving stimulus and thus see the visual path along which it is moving.

Solved Problem 8.2 If you are interviewing for a job and know that the interviewer will be talking to potential candidates all day long, which time slot should you request so that the interviewer is most likely to remember you? Why?

Assuming you do not intend to do something outrageous (the von Restorff effect), you probably should ask for one of the first or last time slots. The reason for this is that items (people) at the start of a list (the **primacy effect**) and items at the end of a list (the **recency effect**) usually are remembered better than are those in the middle of a list. This is the **serial position effect**.

Solved Problem 8.3 Suppose for a hiking trip your friend calls to remind you to pack bug spray, lotion, petroleum jelly, and bandages. You will not be able to resume packing for a little while. What kind of rehearsal should you use to remember these supplies?

Maintenance rehearsal would be if you kept repeating the items until you began to pack again. This would be inefficient. Elaborative rehearsal would involve finding one or more ways to "do something" with the list that would enhance the chances of remembering what was included. You might want to envision a "worst-case scenario" and picture yourself sitting in a blazing sun, surrounded by bugs, trying to repair blister damage on your feet.

Solved Problem 8.4 Identify the "memory tricks" used in the above answer.

Memory is improved if the materials are **organized**. Simply creating a list about the items to be remembered represents a basic level of organization. In addition, picturing the worst-case scenario involves creating **imagery**, another memory aid that improves retention.

Chapter 9
COGNITIVE PROCESSES

Cognitive processes refer to "things that go on in the head." This chapter covers four processes: conceptual thinking, problem solving, decision making, and the development and use of language.

Conceptual Thinking

Thinking is symbolic mediation, or the use of symbols between the presentation of a stimulus and the responses made to it. It is a mental manipulation of the **representation** of information that is inferred from observable behaviors because it cannot be observed directly.

A **symbol** is any stimulus that has become a commonly accepted representation of an object, event, action, or idea. A symbol may take any form or meaning as long as there is general agreement that it stands for a particular thing.

Concepts are symbols that summarize or generalize attributes typical of several objects, events, actions, or ideas. Concepts distinguish between members and nonmembers of the conceptual category on the basis of specified characteristics. They simplify and give structure to what otherwise might be an overly complex world.

Concepts are thought of as falling into **hierarchies** with **superordinate** (the highest), **basic** (intermediate), and **subordinate** (the lowest) levels. Typical speech employs basic-level concepts.

Let's Compare . . . ✔

Level	Object Example	Animal Example
Superordinate	Furniture	Pet
Basic	Chair	Dog
Subordinate	Recliner	Poodle

Ambiguous or "fuzzy" concepts are described by citing a **prototype**, an abstract or idealized concept made up of the "best" characteristics of the category. Prototypes produce high agreement among persons asked to designate which examples fit the category and which do not. Individual examples of the category are called **exemplars**.

Example 9.1 The most likely prototype responses to the question "What is a pet?" are "dog" and "cat," even though other animals are kept as pets. When asked to consider the properties that make a dog or cat the more appropriate response, people will list prototypical features associated with them. If asked about a particular dog or cat, such as a companion from childhood, this would be an exemplar.

Problem Solving

Problem solving occurs when an individual or group establishes a goal and seeks ways to reach that goal. A fairly common problem-solving sequence is as follows: (1) **recognize that there is a problem**, (2) **define the problem accurately**, (3) **produce hypotheses about the problem's solution**, and (4) **test the hypotheses**. This same sequence may apply to both straightforward problems and problems as intricate as a personality difficulty.

Example 9.2 If your boss asks you to travel to "Athens" to evaluate a building, you first must find an appropriate mode of transportation. However, if you interpret the request to mean Athens, Greece, when the intent is to send you to Athens, Ohio, the problem is not defined correctly and no solution you generate is going to work. If you do understand that the city is in Ohio, you can generate possible solutions (hypotheses) involving various ways to get there—drive your own car, fly to the nearest airport and rent a car, take a train—and then test each to determine which is most efficient and cost-effective, selecting the one that seems to fit best with attaining the goal.

One crucial aspect to successful problem solving is producing possible solutions. An **algorithm** is a procedure that guarantees a solution. Computers are programmed with algorithmic procedures. However, algorithms require much energy expenditure, so problem solving often is done using **heuristics**, "rules of thumb" or efficient shortcuts that reduce the complexity of the problem.

Some heuristics are specific to particular kinds of problems, but others are general and may be applied to many situations. These include **means-end analysis**, which compares a current position with the desired end and then tries to find ways to get from the position to the end, and **backward search**, which begins at the end point and works back to a solution. Other heuristics include **availability** and **representativeness**. In availability, solutions are based on how easily an event can be recalled from memory. In representativeness, judgment is based on how much a person or event "fits" a particular category.

Example 9.3 People use representativeness when judging an individual by how closely that person matches the characteristics of a given group. The decision to not hire a teenager with body piercings may be based on "surface characteristics" because the employer believes that teenagers with body piercings are not reliable. The availability heuristic may also be relevant in that the employer may better remember instances of teens with body piercings being troublemakers than instances of "clean-cut" teens being troublemakers.

Creativity can aid problem solving. It is often defined as the structuring of ideas or responses in original yet productive ways. This is also known as **divergent thinking**. In contrast, **convergent thinking** occurs when a problem is solved by calling forth solutions based on already known knowledge.

An example of creativity is generating unusual uses for a common object. A brick may be used to construct a building, but a brick may also be used as a doorstop.

The term **insight** is used to describe the phenomenon in which a problem is posed with no apparent immediate progress in solving it, followed by a sudden solution. Insight seems to involve reconceptualizing the problem to find the solution or strategy that will solve it.

Problem solving is subject to variables that influence other types of performance. Low levels of **motivation** are problematic because an individual with insufficient motivation is unlikely to complete the problem-solving sequence. In addition, a particular motivation may influence a person's attention to only some aspects of the problem.

Past experience may predispose a person to respond in a certain manner. Psychologists distinguish between a **habit**, which implies a long-term tendency to respond a certain way, and **set**, the temporary tendency to respond a particular way. "Set" is an example of an **anchoring heuristic**, in which currently available information is used as the reference point in making a judgment. A form of past experience that has been studied extensively is **functional fixedness**. This occurs when a person is unable to see any other use for an object except its normal or usual one.

Example 9.4 At an outdoor concert that had been threatened by rain, the sun broke through and the temperature rose rapidly. One patron, clutching her umbrella, was heard to say, "I'd be okay if I just had some shade."

She illustrated functional fixedness, being unable to envision opening the umbrella to create the needed shade.

Decision Making

Decision making involves choice. Two variables seem particularly important: the utility of each possible outcome and the probability that each outcome may occur. **Utility** refers to the value the individual places on the outcome. This is sometimes called "weighing one's choices." **Probability** involves judging the odds of various possible outcomes. Misestimations can lead to faulty decision making, as when an unwanted pregnancy or a sexually transmitted disease occurs.

When the decision involves a relatively complex situation, the limits of short-term storage or working memory may influence the process. Inability to hold sufficient information in working memory may cause the decision maker to ignore some important aspects of the situation.

Example 9.5 Weight-conscious people are swayed by advertising that features words associated with being slender. In selling some yogurt products, for example, emphasis is placed on "low-fat" considerations but no mention is made of the relatively high amount of sugar. Consumers may buy the yogurt, ignoring some of the available information because of the distraction of other, possibly misleading information.

Humans do not make the best decisions in all circumstances. One explanation is **satisficing**, the selection of the first alternative encountered that appears to be good enough.

Reasoning is the study of drawing conclusions from information or evidence. Faulty premises can lead to incorrect decisions even when the logic of the reasoning process is sound. **Inductive reasoning** is the process of reaching a conclusion based on specific cases, using available information to reach a general rule (similar to bottom-up processing). **Deductive reasoning** uses general principles to reach specific conclusions (similar to top-down processing). One other kind of reasoning that has been studied extensively is **analogical** reasoning, or thinking that takes an *a* is to *b* as *x* is to *y* format.

> # You Need to Know
>
> - **Hypothesis testing** is an example of deductive reasoning.
> - **Theory development** is an example of inductive reasoning.

Language

Psycholinguists specialize in studying psycholinguistics, or the acquisition, structure, and use of language.

Signs and symbols are both signals that can be used for communication. A **sign** has meaning because of its very nature, while a **symbol** has meaning because a number of people (or other organisms) have chosen to accept that meaning. Any agreed upon designation (a word, drawing, gesture, etc.) may serve as a symbol.

Language in humans consists of **written and spoken forms**. Words are arranged differently, repeated more, and generally take a more casual form in spoken than in written language.

Expressive language is defined as words that convey a message. **Receptive language** defines what is understood from the words used. Interpretation of the words may differ; the message producer may wish to convey one message, while the message receiver may interpret the same words to mean something different.

The study of **word development and usage** has resulted in the following findings: The basic sound components of spoken language are **phonemes**. Young children have the ability to produce the phonemic patterns of many languages but soon learn to limit their patterns to those appropriate to the language being learned. Most analyses suggest that English has about 42 to 45 phonemes. Phonemes in other languages vary from as few as 15 to as many as 85. **Syllables** are what are "heard" or concentrated on by the producer and receiver of a message. They are composed of one or more phonemes. **Morphemes** are the smallest meaningful units of language. Not all syllables are morphemes because not all syllables have meaning when they stand alone. The entire set of morphemes in a language is called the **lexicon**.

Example 9.6 "Wing" is a single-syllable word that is also a morpheme. "Planting" has two syllables, but the "ing" syllable cannot be considered a morpheme because it does not have meaning by itself.

Phonemes, syllables, and morphemes are the structural components of **words**, the symbols used in a language. **Vocabulary** is the repertoire of words an individual knows and uses. Word combinations build **phrases**, which in turn may be developed into **clauses** or **sentences**. Sentences may have several clauses, but when they do, the receiver's typical pattern is to treat each clause separately.

Words are arranged according to **grammatical rules** of language that describe how thoughts can be expressed. How words and phrases can be combined into sentences is referred to as **syntax**. **Semantics** refers to the meaning of words and sentences. The ideas expressed in sentences are **propositions**. It is possible to create arrangements of words that fit the rules of grammar yet convey little or no meaning. The arrangement of words has been called **the surface structure** of the language, while the meaning being transmitted is the **deep structure**.

Example 9.7 The words "dog," "Cathy," "the," and "bought" must be arranged according to the rules of grammar and syntax to form a comprehensible and sensible statement. It is possible to generate more than one meaningful sentence from these words—"Cathy bought the dog" and "The dog bought Cathy"—although the "idea unit" of the first arrangement makes more sense.

Example 9.8 Two sentences such as "Glenn took the test" and "The test was taken by Glenn" have the same deep structure, although their surface structures differ. One could alter the meaning of the second sentence by substituting "purse" for "test." This would leave the surface structure the same but alter the deep structure considerably.

The study of the social rules that help determine the structure (and understanding) of language is **pragmatics**. Context often establishes the form with which an individual expresses an idea and enables interpretation by the receiver.

You Need to Know ✔

There are universal patterns of language acquisition:

- Cooing (producing all phonemes)
- Babbling (producing phonemes of primary language)
- One-word utterances
- Two-word utterances
- Telegraphic speech (producing sentences using only crucial words)
- Sentences (produced at about age 4)

Common errors made by children include **overgeneralization** of rules and **overextension** of words to apply to all exemplars of a category.

The extent to which language influences the study of behavior and mental processes is illustrated by the following topics studied by psycholinguists.

Nature and nurture appear to both play a role in language acquisition. The critical period for language learning and the common language acquisition sequence, both found in children throughout the world, provide evidence for the importance of nature. Regional differences in pronunciation illustrate the importance of nurture.

Bilingual or **multilingual** people are those who speak two or more languages. In instances where both languages have been learned well, perhaps because they were learned sequentially, a bilingual person seems to profit. If one language is replaced by another, there may be decreased cognitive functioning.

Slips of the tongue are inadvertent errors of speech production that generate changed meaning for the thought being expressed. Freud believed these were expressions of hidden or subconscious motivations.

Research on **language development in chimpanzees** has shown that they can learn vocabulary and grammatical understanding using American Sign Language or other symbolic forms. Communication using symbols has occurred between chimpanzees and humans and also has been attempted between chimpanzees—one to another.

Solved Problems

Solved Problem 9.1 Create a mental image of a farm. What was included in your image? Why?

If you included a farmhouse, barn, and some livestock, you are likely to think of these items as prototypical for a farm. Prototypes reach high agreement among people who are asked to designate examples that are representative of the category.

Solved Problem 9.2 At the end of the first week of college, David tells his parents that his roommate's interests are as much like his as "black is to white." What form of reasoning has David shown?

David's statement is in the form of an analogy. Analogical reasoning takes the format of *a* is to *b* as *x* is to *y*, or "David" is to "roommate" as "black" is to "white."

Solved Problem 9.3 An English-speaking person probably will have no difficulty pronouncing the word "jolly," but an Spanish speaker is likely to see that word and say "hoy-yee." Why?

The Spanish language does not make use of phonemes comparable to the sounds represented by "j" and "ll" in English. In fact, such sounds may be virtually unpronounceable for a Spanish speaker not trained in English.

Chapter 10
MOTIVATION AND EMOTION

The Motivation Cycle

Motivation is defined as the conditions which initiate, guide, and maintain behaviors, usually until a goal has been reached or the response has been blocked. The **cycle of motivation** follows a three-part repetitive chain: (1) A **need** creates a **drive**, (2) **operant responses** are made as attempts to reach a goal to satisfy the condition, and (3) once the goal has been reached, **relief** from the motive condition follows. Often the relief is only temporary and the cycle begins again.

91

The strength of motivation can be changed by varying how long it has been since the motive was last satisfied. This period of time represents **deprivation**. Psychologists manipulate deprivation to study motivation. Strength of motivation can also be estimated by observing particular behaviors and inferring the subject's motive condition.

Many motives produce nonproductive responses that require a **behavioral adjustment** so that different operant responses are made and the goal cycle can be completed. Not all satisfiers (goals) are viewed as equally desirable. An organism that prefers a certain goal to others—even when the others would satisfy the motive condition—is exhibiting **goal specificity**.

Principles of Motivation

Instinct refers to an innate condition that provokes a specific response from all members of a species when a distinctive stimulus pattern is present. A **need** is a deficit that can be physiological (warmth) or psychological (achievement). **Drives** are internal psychological states that arise from needs. **Arousal** is thought to be the physiological activation that accompanies drive. Finally, **incentives** refer to external conditions or things that "pull" an organism toward them.

Utility theory combines subjective estimates of desire (drive strength) with the value of desire (incentive strength). Each overall judgment of **expected utility** links a utility estimate with an estimate of the probability that a particular behavior will lead to that goal.

The psychologist Abraham Maslow (1908–1970) developed an ordering or **hierarchy of needs** that formed the basis of a **humanistic theory** of motivation. Maslow's work emphasized that lower-order needs must be satisfied before higher-order needs can be considered.

Remember

Maslow's Hierarchy of Needs:

- Self-actualization
- Esteem
- Love and belongingness
- Safety
- Physiological needs/survival

Some responses to a motive condition may persist even after the original motive ceases to exist. In such a case, the response itself becomes a motive. This is called **functional autonomy**.

Example 10.1 A student initially studies because she wants a good grade. She finds she enjoys psychology, so after the term, she studies psychology because of the enjoyment it brings. She has exhibited functional autonomy.

Psychologists describe an **optimal level of arousal** for the performance of any task. Usually, the best performance occurs at moderate levels of arousal. This is known as the **Yerkes-Dodson law** which is often described as an **inverted-U** relationship between arousal and performance. The exact maximum level of arousal that will yield the best performance varies from task to task. In general, the more difficult the task, the lower the optimal level of arousal.

Arousal serves as the basis for the **activation-arousal theory** of motivation, which proposes that any organism has a typical, normal, appropriate level of arousal and that behavior will be directed toward trying to maintain that level.

Note!

Extraverts may be underaroused compared to their preferred levels of arousal. This may lead them to seek out extra stimulation.

Freud proposed the **psychoanalytic theory** of motivation. He viewed motivation as unconscious and as an expression of aggressive or sexual desires. These desires might be expressed openly or in a symbolic form, such as through dreams or "slips of the tongue."

Social learning theory suggests that prior learning is a major source of motivation. Learning may take place from observing others, and rewards or punishments may be either external or internal.

Types of Motives

Motives can be **primary** or **unlearned** and **secondary** or **learned**. Some motives appear to result from the combined effects of unlearned and learned characteristics, while others cannot be classified.

Some unlearned motives are called **survival motives** because they must be satisfied in order for an organism to continue to live. The list of survival motives is short: hunger, thirst, the need for air, the need to maintain body temperature, the need to relieve fatigue, and the need to eliminate body waste. Many of the body processes that operate to satisfy unlearned motives are automatic. The body regulates itself to maintain an internal physiological balance called **homeostasis**.

Example 10.2 A diet makes use of the body's tendency to make homeostatic adjustments. When people who are overweight reduce their food intake, they create an energy deficit. To make up for this, the body will burn stored fats. This will lower the person's weight. However, not enough food will result in a decrease of metabolic rate in order to conserve energy. This will retard weight loss.

Hunger is the most thoroughly researched unlearned motive. Theories suggest that levels of sugar (glucose) in the blood or levels of fat (lipids) signal the need for food. **Set-point theory** proposes that each person has a preset body weight based on number of fat cells, metabolic rate, or neurochemicals.

Studies of the hypothalamus have shown its involvement in hunger and eating. If the **ventromedial nucleus** is destroyed, an animal will become **hyperphagic** and overeat. If the ventromedial nucleus is activated, a hungry animal will stop eating at once. When the **lateral hypothalamic** area is destroyed, an animal will become **aphagic** and refuse to eat at all. If that area is activated, the animal will eat even if completely satisfied.

Evidence indicates that context is also important in affecting hunger, including the setting for eating and the presentation of the food.

Weight levels at extremes often signal **eating disorders**. Someone who is 20 percent or more overweight is **obese**. Explanations focus on obese individuals' high set points and sensitivity to external stimuli.

Extremely underweight individuals may be suffering from **anorexia nervosa**, a refusal to eat accompanied by denial that the refusal and being underweight are unusual. **Bulimia nervosa** consists of binge eating followed by purging, through vomiting or the use of laxatives. A bulimic usually maintains a normal weight but often suffers from other physiological problems because of the binge-purge cycle. Women are much more likely than men to suffer from anorexia and bulimia.

Learned motives often are called **social motives** because they develop from social interactions and are not necessary for survival.

Need for achievement is one of the most researched learned motives. It likely develops initially because of the social approval of success or the punishment of failure. Much research has been conducted using the **Thematic Apperception Test** (**TAT**; see Chapter 11). The TAT presents a series of ambiguous pictures about which a person is asked to tell stories. These may reveal the subject's motivations, including the need for achievement. Need for achievement predicts the difficulty of tasks that people undertake. People with a high need for achievement choose moderately difficult tasks. Individuals low in the need to achieve select very easy or difficult tasks, ensuring success or guaranteeing failure.

The **need for dominance** or **power** is satisfied by being able to direct others' behaviors through persuasion, suggestion, command, or other means. The choice of careers, such as management and teaching, and collecting possessions that reflect power are among the characteristics that are correlated with the need for dominance.

Another highly researched learned motive is the **need for affiliation** with others through friendship or group membership. Closely related is the motive for **dependency**, or reliance on others.

The **need to relieve anxiety** may serve as a motive condition, causing a person to seek responses that will reduce anxiety. Rather than seeking something positive, an anxious person is motivated to get away from something negative.

Let's Compare . . . ✔

- **Approach motives** refer to attaining desirable goals.
- **Avoidance motives** refer to avoiding undesirable goals.

Sexual motivation includes unlearned and learned characteristics. Research on sexual responses has shown that women and men experience a similar sequence: **excitement**, **plateau**, **orgasm**, and a **refractory period**. Standards of attractiveness and acceptable sexual practices are a function of social learning. The cognitive processes accompanying sexual motivation are learned **sexual scripts**, mental representations of ways in which sexual behaviors should be enacted.

The apparent need of the young to have soft, warm, cuddly things to which they may cling is called **contact comfort**, a motive with origins that remain matters of debate.

Conflict

Simultaneous motives that are incompatible are **conflicts**. One of the milder and more easily resolved is the **approach-approach conflict**, a situation in which a person must choose between two or more positively valued objects. An **avoidance-avoidance conflict** occurs when a person is confronted with a choice between two or more negatively valued objects. Occasionally the person will withdraw from the situation rather than choose. An **approach-avoidance conflict** occurs when a single object has both positive and negative qualities. The relative strengths of these must be weighed in order for resolution to occur.

Example 10.3 Someone on a diet is confronted with a dessert menu. This person may see each choice as both positive (it will taste good) and negative (it has many calories). The menu creates **multiple approach-avoidance conflicts** because there are multiple stimuli.

General Characteristics of Emotions

Emotion is a complex state that generally is characterized by heightened arousal and personal feelings. Because the judgment that an emotion exists is a subjective matter, it is often helpful to identify the stimulus that generated the response.

An athlete's tears may be due to the thrill of victory or the agony of defeat.

Emotional reactions may provoke additional responses so that emotion serves as a motivator.

Several indicators of emotion are used in psychological research, including self-reports of the person, observed behaviors (gestures, postures, and facial expressions), and physiological reactions. Changes in heart rate, blood pressure, breathing, pupil dilation, and electrodermal activity (EDA or galvanic skin response, GSR) may all be indicators of emotion.

Two cautions about observing or interpreting emotions are important. First, attributing human characteristics or emotions to lower organisms is **anthropomorphism**. This should be avoided, especially when a more simple explanation is sufficient. A simple, or **parsimonious**, explanation is preferable to a more complicated one—in all of psychology, not just in studies of emotion.

Example 10.4 A dog given food will wag its tail. It is more appropriate to refer to the dog's response as tail wagging than to say that the dog is "happy."

Basic Types of Emotions

Psychologists generally agree that emotions can be classified on the dimensions of pleasant-unpleasant and mild-extreme, but the number of labels for emotion categories ranges depending on the category and the language studied. Some emotions about which many researchers agree are included below.

Fear-producing stimuli change in importance as a person matures. What is sudden, unexpected, and frightening to a child may not be fear-provoking to an adult and vice versa. Fear and **anxiety** are distinguished on the basis of the specificity of the stimulus that provokes the response. Fear, unlike anxiety, is thought to arise from a well-defined stimulus. Extreme fears, which may result from classical conditioning, are called **phobias**.

The emotional reactions associated with **anger** may vary from "worked up" to infuriated. Such reactions are provoked by displeasing or frustrating stimuli that block successful goal attainment, especially if they are seen as intentional. Research has shown that rather than relieving anger, the expression of anger may intensify it.

Grief or sorrow reactions are provoked by stimuli that involve permanent separation from a loved one or an irreconcilable hurt. Milder forms of this may be labeled as **sadness**.

Pleasure ranges from reactions of delight to ecstatic experiences of joy or love. Pleasure reactions are generated by the presence of favorable stimuli that lead to desired goals. Expressions of pleasure may take diverse forms, such as smiling or kissing.

Many emotional situations can be described as **variations** or **combinations** of more basic emotions. Other ways to study emotions include investigating cultural or other situational variables involved in producing emotions.

Theories of Emotion

The **James-Lange theory**, named for William James and Carl Lange, states that stimuli that produce bodily changes generate felt emotions. Thus, this theory suggests that emotions result from interpretations of physical reactions.

Walter Cannon and Philip Bard recognized that identical bodily states could not logically cause different emotions. **The Cannon-Bard theory** suggests that when an emotion-producing stimulus is received in the brain, centers in the thalamus and hypothalamus send out simultaneous signals to muscles, organs, and the cortex. The muscle and organ responses constitute physiological reactions to the emotion, while the cortex interprets the signals as emotion. Thus, physiological and psychological reactions occur at the same time.

More recent work has stressed the interaction of cognitive and physiological influences. The **two-factor theory of emotion** relies upon physiological arousal and labeling of that arousal. This theory has been criticized because the same kind of arousal could be associated with a number of different emotional reactions. Richard Lazarus distinguished between **primary appraisal**, an initial assessment of how an event may affect well-being, and **secondary appraisal**, an evaluation of the resources available for coping.

Example 10.5 Anger may result if a person appraises a car accident as the fault of another driver. Sadness might be experienced instead if the appraisal does not lead to an attribution of fault. Anger may be tempered by the secondary appraisal that the accident is relatively unimportant, resulting in mere irritation rather than more intense anger.

Robert Zajonc has argued that emotion and cognition are separate processes and that appraisal is not necessary for experiencing emotion. As these multiple theories illustrate, it is unlikely that any single theory of emotion is going to be accepted without question.

Special Topics in Emotion

Research on emotions has led to several intriguing areas of investigation. According to the **facial feedback hypothesis**, facial expressions of emotion contribute to the initiation or modification of emotional experiences.

Example 10.6 In one study, subjects were asked to hold a pen in their teeth (forcing a smile) or with their lips (forcing a nonsmiling expression). While doing this, the subjects were asked to rate the humor of cartoons. Those forced to "smile" rated the cartoons as funnier than the others who maintained the nonsmiling expression.

Although studies have not been able to establish distinct patterns of physiological indicators of emotion, the theory of **lie detection** depends on the idea that a person telling a lie experiences general emotional arousal. Thus, physiological indicators of emotion sometimes can be used to judge whether a person is telling the truth.

Some people may come to expect that unpleasant experiences in their lives are inevitable. These people may accept what are considered unalterable consequences, demonstrating **learned helplessness** in other situations.

Psychosomatic illnesses are real physical problems (e.g., high blood pressure) that are linked with psychological variables, such as stress and conflict. **Somatoform disorders** are characterized by the presence of one or more symptoms of a physical dysfunction (e.g., blindness) for which no organic cause can be found.

Solved Problems

Solved Problem 10.1 Your child has been acting up in class, misbehaving until the teacher has to interrupt the class activities to correct your child. The teacher asks you why the child persists in misbehaving. Having just studied this chapter, you answer, "It's just an example of the motivation cycle." Explain.

Perhaps the child needs attention or social recognition from the teacher. If this is lacking in everyday activities, the need continues to grow until the child has to find a way to get attention. Disruption is the operant response; the goal is temporarily satisfied and does not reappear until the motive strength has increased again.

Solved Problem 10.2 Envy is a common label for an emotional reaction. Show how the concept of envy may be viewed as a combination of some "basic" emotions.

Envy implies wishing to have what someone else has. This may have resulted from fear of not being able to attain the goal or frustration and the resultant anger from wanting something unobtainable.

Chapter 11

PSYCHOLOGICAL TESTING AND INDIVIDUAL DIFFERENCES

In This Chapter:

- ✔ *Characteristics of a Good Test*
- ✔ *Measuring Intelligence*
- ✔ *Composition of Intelligence*
- ✔ *Assessing Personality*
- ✔ *Other Testing Areas*
- ✔ *Testing Concerns*
- ✔ *Solved Problems*

The construction and use of tests to measure **samples of behavior** is referred to as **psychometrics**.

Characteristics of a Good Test

Reliability is the consistency with which a result can be obtained. **Parallel form** reliability is indicated by the correlation between results from two equivalent forms of a test. When only one form is available, the items are divided in half and the correlation between results obtained from the two halves measures **split-half** reliability. Reliability may also be examined over time and across observers of a behavior.

Validity means that a test measures what it claims to measure. In **criterion validity**, a correlation between test results and a different measure of the behavior assessed by the test is calculated. When this is done with measures that currently exist, it is called **concurrent validity**; when test results are correlated with performance at a later time, it is **predictive validity**. On occasion, validity is estimated when experts in the field judge how well a test appears to measure the areas being tested; this is **content-related validity**. Improper use of tests may lead to inaccurate predictions and faulty counseling or advice.

Remember

- A test may be reliable but not valid if it measures something consistently but does not measure what it claims to measure.
- A test can be valid but not reliable. If a test measures what it claims to measure, it must do so reliably.

Standardization refers to how testing is conducted. All aspects of the testing procedure—administration of the test, scoring, evaluation of results—should follow the same procedures. Without standardization, differences among the performances of the subjects may be the result of variations in test procedures and not differences among subjects.

Standardization also refers to the establishment of **norms**, which are scores obtained from groups of people who have taken the test. Then the performances of others can be compared to the norms. Although norms are frequently helpful in interpreting the results of tests, they can sometimes be misleading. In such cases, it may be better to use a **criterion**, or **absolute standard**, to evaluate performance.

Objectivity means that an examiner's biases play no role in observation or assessment.

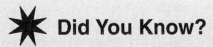

Did You Know?

An examiner's expectancies can influence actual performance on many different types of tests.

Measuring Intelligence

The first standard measurements of intelligence were developed in Paris in the early 1900s by Alfred Binet. His test was later revised by Lewis Terman of Stanford University and was released in 1916 as the Stanford-Binet Intelligence Test. A revised form is still in use today.

No single **definition of intelligence** is accepted. Phrases commonly found in current definitions include "goal-directed," "adaptive behavior," and "ability to understand the world," characteristics that allow for problem solving and thinking rationally. Some psychologists simply assert that intelligence is whatever intelligence tests measure.

The Stanford-Binet test makes use of the concept of **mental age** (**MA**). This refers to the age required for many people to complete particular items successfully. Because not all subjects who achieve the same mental age on a test are the same age, a ratio was developed. This is called the **intelligence quotient** (**IQ**) and is equal to the value of MA divided by **chronological** (actual) **age** (**CA**), multiplied by 100.

Example 11.1 Ike and Tina obtained an MA of 9 years (108 months) on an IQ test. Ike is 9 years old; Tina is 6 years, 9 months old. Applying the above formula, Ike's IQ is 100, while Tina's is about 133.

Difficulties with this **ratio IQ** arose as subjects approached adulthood. There was no way for it to measure mental age in a way that could take into account the ever-increasing chronological age of a subject. As a result, David Wechsler proposed a **deviation IQ**, basing the reported IQ value on the normal probability curve. The Wechsler tests of intelligence have a mean IQ of 100 and a standard deviation (*SD*) of 15. IQ is determined by comparing a subject's performance to the norms from the subject's age group.

Example 11.2 A person scoring 115 is in the 84th percentile compared to the standardization norms, while the percentile for someone scoring 70 is 2.5 (see Chapter 2 for the statistical procedures).

Persons who obtain scores that differ from the mean by two or more *SD*s are **exceptional subjects**. People with scores two or more *SD*s below the mean are **mentally retarded**, while those with scores two or more *SD*s above the mean are **gifted**.

Subgroups within the category of mental retardation have been defined. These subgroups and their IQ cutoff points are as follows:

70–50: Mildly retarded (educable)
49–35: Moderately retarded (trainable)
34–20: Severely retarded (minimal skills)
19–0: Profoundly retarded (custodial care)

Retardation may result from any number of factors. These include poor prenatal nutrition or ingestion of toxins, postnatal brain trauma, and extra chromosomal material, as in **Down syndrome**. In the United States, legislation stipulates that retarded children be educated in the **least restricted environment**. This has been referred to as **mainstreaming**, or integration into regular classrooms when possible.

Gifted people are not divided into further subgroupings. Subjects with very high IQ scores (values of 180 or more) may have adjustment difficulties. However, research indicates that the gifted generally are better adjusted and healthier than are people with average IQ scores.

Genetic effects that lead to individual differences in IQ scores are represented by the **heritability coefficient**. Possible values range from 0 (heredity has no effect on the variation in IQ scores), to 1 (variation among people in IQ scores can be attributed exclusively to heredity). Estimates of heritability coefficients have ranged from .3 to .8.

Example 11.3 Studies of identical twins placed in separate homes must take into account the fact that adoption or foster care agencies often try to pick homes that are comparable. It is likely that environmental influences in both homes are similar, so that a high heritability coefficient between identical twins who have been reared apart may misrepresent the actual effects.

Composition of Intelligence

Developmental psychology, information-processing theory, and statistical practices are used to identify the structure of intelligence.

The statistical technique often used is **factor analysis**. The study of performance of various tasks allows psychologists to identify characteristics of intelligence (types of tasks) that are correlated. Early research showed that many different tasks appeared to share a common base (because performance on them was correlated). Charles Spearman called this **g factor**, or **general intelligence factor**. L. L. Thurstone proposed that g linked seven basic characteristics of intelligence he identified using factor analysis. These are as follows:

- **Verbal comprehension**: definition and understanding of words
- **Word fluency**: thinking of words rapidly
- **Number**: doing arithmetic problems
- **Space**: understanding spatial relationships
- **Rote memory**: memorization and recall
- **Perceptual**: grasping similarities, differences, and details in objects
- **Reasoning**: understanding concepts for problem solving

Raymond Cattell suggested two general intelligences: **Fluid intelligence** is the ability to reason abstractly, think creatively, or understand complex relationships, and it seems to be influenced by heredity. **Crystallized intelligence** represents what a person has learned from experience; it indicates the influences of the environment.

The developmental sequence of cognitive growth proposed by Piaget has been used to understand intelligence. Using this approach, intelligence is estimated by comparing the particular characteristics of a person with the sequence proposed by Piaget.

There may be **multiple intelligences** of different types. Howard Gardner proposed eight types, noting that any task might involve several of these working together:

- **Musical intelligence**: performing tasks related to music
- **Bodily kinesthetic intelligence**: using the body to solve problems
- **Logical-mathematical intelligence**: scientific problem solving
- **Linguistic intelligence**: production and use of language
- **Spatial intelligence**: spatial relationships
- **Interpersonal intelligence**: interacting with others
- **Intrapersonal intelligence**: assessing one's own feelings and emotions
- **Naturalistic intelligence**: making distinctions in the natural world

Robert Sternberg developed a **triarchic theory of intelligence**. The **componential** aspect of intelligence is used in analyzing information. **Experiential** intelligence is how well previous learning is used to solve problems, while **contextual** intelligence involves using intelligence to address environmental demands, also conceptualized as **practical** intelligence. Recently, Sternberg proposed the concept of **successful** intelligence, defined in terms of one's ability to achieve success in life according to both personal and sociocultural standards.

Example 11.**4** Traditional concepts of intelligence have been of academic intelligence. Tests now are being developed to assess practical or contextual intelligence. Respondents indicate the likelihood of different responses to everyday situations, such as to a job problem.

John Carroll suggested a hierarchical model of cognitive, rather than intellectual, abilities. At the base are **narrow abilities** acquired in response to environmental pressures. At the second level are **broad abilities**, such as learning, verbal fluency, and memory, that are thought to result from an interaction of environmental and hereditary influences. At the top of the hierarchy is **g**, or **general cognitive ability**, which is attributed primarily to genetic influences.

Assessing Personality

Personality tests are designed to determine what is typical of a person.

They are often related to a theory about personality.

Questionnaires to which respondents indicate answers such as "yes," "agree," and "disagree" are **self-report tests**. Perhaps the best known is the **Minnesota Multiphasic Personality Inventory-2** (**MMPI-2**), which consists of 567 items about opinions, moods, and physical and psychological health. The MMPI-2 includes 10 subscales, plus 3 checks for the validity of responses (including a "lie scale" that indicates when a respondent falsifies responses, perhaps trying to look good). Another self-report method is the **adjective checklist**, from which a person picks adjectives he or she believes are self-descriptive.

In **projective personality tests**, the subject is presented with ambiguous stimuli and asked for a description of or a story about each. The theory is that a person will reveal some personality characteristics by projecting them onto the stimulus provided. The two most widely known tests are the **Thematic Apperception Test** (**TAT**), which uses 20 monochrome pictures, and the **Rorschach Test**, which uses 10 inkblots, some of which have color. Scoring guidelines have been developed to help maintain objectivity.

Behavioral assessments may be done in a naturalistic setting such as home, work, or school. Some are conducted in previously planned situations, in which the subject reacts to controlled conditions.

Interviews are face-to-face encounters between people. They give an interviewer an opportunity to expand on questions or probe answers. Psychotherapy can be considered a special form of interview assessment. Freud employed **free association** (letting each thought simply lead to the next) as a means of assessment.

Other Testing Areas

Tests designed to measure what a person has accomplished are **achievement tests**. Tests designed to predict what a person may accomplish in the future are **aptitude tests**. Both are based on the concept of **ability**, a person's potential for acquiring a skill. **Scholastic** aptitude tests are intended to predict success in schools. **Vocational** tests are intended to estimate success in employment situations.

Example 11.5 Scholastic aptitude tests predict well how a student may respond to additional academic training. However, such a test may be inappropriate for gauging psychomotor abilities, for which tests of manual dexterity or coordination should be used. Psychologists have to design a testing program suited to the particular task being predicted.

Tests related to employment also may be categorized as interest or screening tests. **Interest tests** propose careers consistent with a person's likes and dislikes. **Screening tests** are intended to identify applicants who show the "best fit" for a job.

A **creative act** is one which is original and useful. Creative thinking often is referred to as **divergent thinking**; however, even divergent thinking does not guarantee creative thinking. Academic intelligence is related to creativity, but several other characteristics better differentiate creative from noncreative people. In general, a creative person is flexible in thinking, is interested in complex and novel ideas, is aesthetically sensitive, shows a complex personality pattern, and shows a willingness to take risks.

Measures of creativity share the aim of evaluating unique or novel solutions to problems. These include: (1) **unusual uses tests** (generate unusual uses for an object), (2) **remote association tests** (find an association common to several stimulus words), (3) **anagram tests** (find as many small words as possible from a larger stimulus word), and (4) **drawing completion tests** (finish a partial drawing).

Example 11.6 In a drawing completion test, the subject may be asked to complete a drawing, such as the one that appears in Figure 11-1 (a), in any way he or she wants. Response (b) might indicate a lack of creativity, while response (c) would be considered creative.

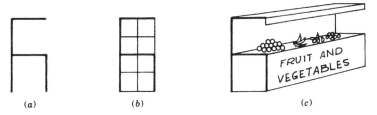

(a)   (b)   (c)

Figure 11-1 A sample drawing completion test item.

Testing Concerns

There has been growing concern about the **ethics of testing** in adminis-tration, scoring, interpretation, and reporting of results. One serious con-cern has been about privacy. Privacy is invaded if the results of a test are revealed without the consent of the test subject.

Concerns have also been raised about **test fairness**. Attempts have been made to develop culture-free or culture-fair tests, with limited suc-cess. Psychologists must realize the limitations of test scores and not rely on them exclusively when making decisions about individuals.

Psychologists sometimes combine information from more than one test. This is referred to as a **test battery**.

Many forms of psychological tests, including intelligence tests, can be administered either to individuals or groups. **Individual tests** are viewed as more sensitive measures than **group tests** and are used when subjects' motivations are suspect. However, individual tests are costly and require more time and administrator training.

Solved Problems

Solved Problem 11.1 A famous jazz group recorded an album in which many of the songs involved intricate rhythms, such as two players per-forming music with four beats per measure while the other two simulta-neously played music with three beats per measure. Using Gardner's mul-tiple intelligences model, select those that might have been involved in this accomplishment.

Certainly musical intelligence is important. In addition, the intrica-cy of the rhythms probably involves logical-mathematical intelligence, while the interactions necessary among the musicians would require in-terpersonal intelligence. Bodily kinesthetic intelligence might be in-volved in the actual playing.

Solved Problem 11.2 What are the properties of culture-free and culture-fair tests?

In a culture-free test, the items are selected so that cultural differ-ences will not influence a subject's response. In culture-fair tests, the items are expressed using terms understandable to members of the subject's culture. These tests do not produce results significantly different from those in standard psychological testing. Furthermore, there is probably no such thing as a truly culture-free or culture-fair test.

Chapter 12
PERSONALITY
PRINCIPLES

<small>IN THIS CHAPTER:</small>

- ✔ *General Factors Influencing Personality*
- ✔ *Freud's Theory of Personality*
- ✔ *Other Psychodynamic Theories*
- ✔ *Dispositional Theories of Personality*
- ✔ *Learning Theories of Personality*
- ✔ *Humanistic Theories of Personality*
- ✔ *Cross-Cultural Differences in Personality*
- ✔ *Solved Problems*

General Factors Influencing Personality

Personality consists of enduring attributes that describe or cause a person's behavior. A person's **environmental experiences** affect the development of personality characteristics. These experiences may be **unique** to one person or **common** to many people.

Genetic patterns influence personality. Inherited brain damage or birth defects may have a pronounced influence. Additionally, somatic (body) factors such as height, weight, and the functioning of sense organs may affect personality development.

The combined effects of **heredity** and **environment** influence many personality attributes. As with other characteristics, the closer the relationship of two people, the more likely it is that their personality characteristics will be similar.

Freud's Theory of Personality

Psychodynamic theory was developed from Freud's attempts to design therapeutic techniques. Important in Freud's approach was his emphasis on the influence of the **unconscious**, an internal structure of the mind, the activity of which was outside normal awareness. This differed from the **conscious** or **preconscious**, which contained thoughts of which one is aware or that can be brought readily into awareness. Activities of the unconscious may influence behaviors despite the lack of awareness of these unconscious effects.

Freud believed that personality was motivated by a fundamental drive called **libido**. He emphasized the sexual nature of libido and believed that many of the goals people sought could be explained by reference to the pursuit of pleasure.

Freud proposed that personality had three components: id, ego, and superego. The **id** is the most primitive or instinctive part of personality. The id operates according to the **pleasure principle**, seeking pleasure and avoiding pain regardless of societal beliefs or restraints. The **ego** is the problem-solving part of personality, which operates according to the **reality principle**. The ego seeks pleasure and avoids pain in rational ways approved of by society. The **superego** reminds the person of ideal and unacceptable behaviors. **Conscience** is found in the superego.

Example 12.1 Shopping in a supermarket, Louise, her teenage son, and her 1-year-old daughter stop in the fruit aisle. The daughter grabs a strawberry and begins munching happily; she seeks pleasure and satisfies the motive. The son spots some grapes, thinks that everybody "rips off" the store a little, takes a small handful, and starts eating. Louise sees some peaches she would like but they are expensive. She considers putting a few in her pocket. However, she realizes this would be dishonest and does without the peaches. Louise's actions represent superego influence, her son seems to have been under ego control, and her daughter was under the control of the id.

Freud thought that personality developed through five **psychosexual stages**, during which libidinal energy found a particular focus. If the individual progressed through each stage without difficulties, a mature adult expression of libidinal energy could be achieved. Disturbances in the form of frustration or excessive gratification at one of the stages could lead to **fixation**, in which some of the libidinal energy of the adult would have to be used to satisfy responses appropriate to the earlier stage rather than responses appropriate for an adult.

The first psychosexual stage is the **oral stage** (0–2 years). Libidinal energy centers on oral activities, particularly feeding and weaning. Fixation at this stage means that a high level of oral activity may be shown by an adult.

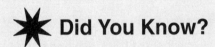

✴ Did You Know?

Smoking and fingernail biting may result from fixation at the oral stage.

In the **anal stage** (2–4 years) libidinal energy is focused on the external conflicts created by toilet training. Fixation at this stage may result in adult difficulties with the giving or withholding of love or approval, stubbornness, and conflicts between neatness and sloppiness.

In the **phallic stage** (4–5 years), the source of libidinal pleasure is the genitalia. Characteristic behaviors include exploration of the genitals and interest in anatomic differences between the sexes. Inability to achieve adult sexuality may result from fixation at the phallic stage. Freud believed this was the period when the **Oedipal complex** (for boys) and the **Electra complex** (for girls) had to be resolved. He proposed that a child has sexual desires for the parent of the opposite sex and feels rivalry with the parent of the same sex. Fear of punishment causes the child to identify with the parent of the same sex and adopt similar behaviors.

Failure to complete this identification process may result in incomplete gender identity and affect responses in situations involving authority (an underdeveloped conscience) or sex-role-appropriate behaviors.

During the **latency stage** libidinal energies are weak, and most behaviors center on interaction with same-sex peers.

At puberty, a person enters the final **genital stage** of development. Libidinal energies are rearoused, and the individual attempts to achieve adult sexuality. If there have been difficulties at other stages, the giving and receiving of mature love may be difficult to achieve.

Freud proposed that a person develops and uses **ego defense mechanisms** to protect the self from anxiety. The main defense mechanism is **repression**, which occurs when the individual "forgets" anxiety-producing memories or keeps unacceptable desires from surfacing in the conscious. Sustained repression requires psychic energy, and a person may devote a large portion of available energy to it. This could result in an abnormal personality pattern. Other defense mechanisms include: **rationalization, projection, displacement, sublimation, regression, and denial**.

Let's Compare ... ✔

Defense	Example
Projection	Lead fight against pornography
Sublimation	Play ice hockey
Regression	Resume thumb-sucking

Other Psychodynamic Theories

Theories related to Freud's work were developed by others, sometimes called **neo-Freudians**. **Carl Jung** placed more emphasis on current events than on childhood experiences and on social motives than on sexual drives. Jung's **analytical psychology** also emphasized spiritual needs and thoughts about the future. Jung's concept of the unconscious included the **personal unconscious** (similar to the Freudian unconscious) and the **collective unconscious**, which is inherited. The collective unconscious carries **archetypes** or tendencies developed over generations that become typical of all people.

 Alfred Adler also stressed social motivation. The key to personality was striving for superiority to compensate for real or imagined deficiencies. Adler recognized that society sometimes reinforces deficiencies, which could lead to an **inferiority complex**.

 Erik Erikson developed an eight-stage theory characterized by a **crisis** to be resolved at each stage. The stages and crises are:

- **Oral-sensory stage**: trust versus mistrust
- **Muscular-anal stage**: autonomy versus doubt
- **Locomotor-genital stage**: initiative versus guilt
- **Latency stage**: industry versus inferiority
- **Puberty and adolescence**: identity versus role confusion
- **Early adulthood**: intimacy versus isolation
- **Young and middle adulthood**: generativity versus self-absorption
- **Mature adulthood**: integrity versus despair

Example 12.2 In Erikson's second stage, a child might have the opportunity to use and control musculature when feeding himself. If successful, the child develops a sense of independence; if unsuccessful, a sense of doubt may develop. The feeling that develops generalizes to affect later psychological development.

 Object relations theory combines a focus on the ego with an emphasis on social relations. **Object** refers to the people with whom an infant forms attachments. Personality development is thought to be influenced by how a child relates to others.

Dispositional Theories of Personality

Identifying dominant, consistent, and enduring qualities of people is the basis of **dispositional** or **trait theories** of personality. **Factor analysis** contributes to decisions about which characteristics to emphasize. The selection of the original items used in factor analysis is crucial, because the resulting factors depend on the material used.

Gordon Allport studied dictionary words used to describe people. Allport called a single characteristic that determines behavior in almost all situations a **cardinal trait**. **Central traits** are not as broad, but apply in many situations. Less consistent and less generalized characteristics are **secondary traits**.

Raymond Cattell used factor analysis to identify 16 **primary** or **source traits** of personality. He developed the "16-PF" test to measure an individual's standing on each of these traits.

People in different cultures, age groups, and occupations consistently tend to use five major traits to describe personality. These have been called the "**big five**" and are as follows:

- **Extraversion**: outgoing, affectionate, fun-loving—not shy
- **Agreeableness**: helpful, cooperative—not hostile or self-centered
- **Conscientiousness**: dependable, organized—not careless or impulsive
- **Openness to experience**: imaginative, flexible—not rigid
- **Neuroticism**: anxious, unstable—not calm or well-adjusted

---

Don't Forget

The big five traits can be remembered using an acronym as a mnemonic: O-C-E-A-N.

Another dispositional approach focuses on biological influences on behavior due to the configuration of the nervous system, the activity of the endocrine glands and their hormones, or neurotransmitters activity. These produce differences in **temperament**, an innate disposition that predisposes mood and activity levels.

Learning Theories of Personality

B. F. Skinner proposed a **reinforcement approach**—that personality was nothing more than the sum of learned behavior patterns made in response to environmental contingencies. If a pattern is reinforced consistently, then the person repeats the pattern consistently.

Julian Rotter's social-cognitive theory emphasized cognitive interpretations and expectancies. A person's interpretation of an event affects how a person responds to the event. Special importance is given to **locus of control**, the generalized expectancy that behaviors are determined by one's own efforts (**internal locus of control**) or by environmental factors beyond one's control (**external locus of control**). Rotter developed the I-E scale to measure these expectancies.

Example 12.3 A person with an internal locus of control is likely to think that hard work and skills make job success possible. A person with an external locus of control attributes job success to a friendly boss, good luck, or fate.

Albert Bandura stresses the effects of modeling, imitation, and observational learning on personality. Two concepts are important to Bandura's work: reciprocal determinism and **self-efficacy** (competence beliefs in specific settings). **Reciprocal determinism** refers to the mutually causal relationships among behavioral variables, environmental variables, and person/cognitive variables. Self-efficacy beliefs are correlated with successful performance in many domains.

Humanistic Theories of Personality

Humanistic theories of personality emphasize the whole person and helping people achieve their full potential. Subjective experience and feelings are important, as is **personal responsibility** for behavior.

Abraham Maslow's work forms much of the basis for humanistic approaches to personality. His hierarchy of motives culminated with self-actualization, a state in which people reach ultimate fulfillment that is thought to be the driving force of personality.

Carl Rogers developed a **self theory** stressing a person's wish to realize potentialities. This means that people would live in perfect accord with themselves and others. Full realization depends on the atmosphere in which one grows up. Best is an atmosphere of **unconditional positive regard**, in which individuals are valued for who they are. Rogers found that many people are raised with **conditional positive regard**, in which approval and respect are contingent on behavior. Personality maladjustment occurs when there is a difference between a person's self-image and reality. When a person is unable to incorporate new experiences into his or her self-image, anxiety may result, leading to defenses against seeing the truth.

Cross-Cultural Differences in Personality

Because personality results from the totality of experiences, there is no way to make valid comparisons across different cultural settings. Psychologists try to separate general and specific patterns of personality, suggesting that there are general patterns that cross cultural boundaries but that other characteristics depend on the culture in which a person is raised. This is an area of continuing research.

Example 12.4 Cultures such as that in the United States place great emphasis on the self or individual potential (**individualism**), while other cultures emphasize the group (**collectivism**). Personality patterns that emerge in the different cultures reflect this difference.

Solved Problems

Solved Problem 12.1 Dr. Lindquist asks all of her students to respond to an adjective list by rating items they think are descriptive of themselves. Dr. Lindquist then uses these responses to show the students how a factor analysis is conducted. What does she say?

First, the analysis is based on correlations between items on the list. If students rated one item high, did they also rate another similar item high? If they did not rate the first one high, did they not give a high rating to the second? When such correlational checks are completed, common factors or traits can be identified.

Second, a factor analysis is only as complete as the items in the list.

If Dr. Lindquist purposely left out all adjectives related to extraversion, she can show the class that the analysis totally missed that characteristic.

Solved Problem 12.2 "Rachel is a brat when she is put to bed. She cries and whines; sometimes we have to go in three times to get her settled." What would Skinner say about Rachel?

Rachel apparently has found a way to get her parents' attention. She gets reinforced repeatedly for crying and whining: They reappear and spend more time with her. She develops that personality pattern because it works.

Chapter 13
ABNORMAL PERSONALITY PATTERNS

Definition of Abnormal Personality Patterns

Behaviors that produce significant and persistent discomfort or upset represent **abnormal personality patterns**. Other terms include "mental illness" and "emotional disturbance." Both the **quantity** (frequency) and **quality** (intensity) of behavior must be considered in judging whether a behavior is abnormal. Personal and social settings also determine whether a pattern is considered abnormal.

Example 13.1 A temporary anxiety about giving a public speech would be normal, while constant anxiety about life in general would be classified as abnormal.

The onset of abnormal behavior seems to result from an interaction between a person's background (heredity and experiences) and the current environment. The background variables are called **predisposing factors**. The stimuli that ultimately initiate the abnormal pattern are called **precipitating factors**.

Abnormal patterns are defined by the *Diagnostic and Statistical Manual of Mental Disorders* (*DSM-IV-TR*), published by the American Psychiatric Association. Using five separate dimensions, or **axes**, *DSM-IV* provides a means for classifying behaviors in more than 200 separate diagnostic categories. It is primarily descriptive; it does not try to specify a cause for a problem behavior.

Perspectives on Abnormal Behaviors

Biomedical models emphasize the influence of bodily functions on abnormality. Disease, genetic inheritance, or the condition of a person's nervous system may be the sources of abnormal behavior. Therapies based on biomedical models often make use of drugs or surgery.

Psychologists who base their approach on the work of Freud believe that abnormal behaviors result from conflicts in the unconscious. Therapies based on the **psychodynamic model** stress becoming aware of the unconscious processes and thus resolving the conflicts.

The **behavioral model** attributes abnormal

patterns to learning. Abnormal responses are acquired because of reinforcement, observation, and imitation. Therapies based on this model may make use of the principles of classical or operant conditioning and modeling.

The **humanistic model** stresses a person's responsibility for behavior. Abnormal patterns arise from conflict between a person's self-image and the reality of a situation. Therapy based on this model focuses on helping a person understand and find ways to reach the self-image that allows appropriate interactions with others.

The **cognitive model** focuses on beliefs and biases related to a person's feelings of self-worth, view of the world, and conceptualization of the future, stressing the idea that abnormal patterns result from negative approaches to one or more of these factors. Therapy tries to change the client's thinking by teaching new, adaptive beliefs.

You Need to Know

The predominant model of mental disorders is the biopsychosocial model; biological, psychological, and social variables all contribute to abnormality.

Anxiety Disorders

Intense and prolonged anxiety with no obvious external cause is an **anxiety disorder**.

Panic disorders are characterized by sudden, unexplained attacks of fear that last up to several hours. People with panic disorders may experience difficulty breathing, chest pain, sweating, trembling, and even the fear of dying or "going crazy." There is evidence that hereditary biological factors may be involved.

Phobic disorders are intense fears of a specific situation or an object. Phobias are likely the result of classical conditioning or displacement, in which the fear of one thing is a symbolic fear of something else.

Some people think thoughts (**obsessions**) or perform actions (**compulsions**) in a repetitive and disturbing fashion. Often, obsessive thoughts are linked to and seem to produce compulsive behaviors (**obsessive-compulsive disorder**).

Example 13.2 Obsessive compulsive behavior can be seen in a person who is plagued by worries that the doors to the office have not been locked and who must return repeatedly to check.

Generalized anxiety disorder is characterized by long-term, persistent anxiety without a clear cause. This kind of anxiety often leads to disorganized behavior and frequently produces physiological symptoms such as muscle tension, headaches, dizziness, and insomnia.

Dissociative Disorders

Dissociative disorders involve a disturbance of personal memories or identity that may help one escape from anxiety-producing situations.

The partial or total forgetting of some past experiences, usually after a stressful event, is called **dissociative amnesia**. The cause is psychological; for example, when someone witnesses a traumatic accident and is unable to remember it or the activities that followed.

Dissociative fugue is characterized by "walking away" from one's life for periods of time that may range from hours to years. The individual often assumes a new identity and, if subsequent recovery occurs, remembers nothing about the fugue period.

Dissociative identity disorder is popularly referred to as **multiple personality disorder**. This involves a person with more than one well-defined personality. Transition from one personality to another often occurs rapidly, with changed voice and expressions. One personality may know of another, even to the point of friendship or rivalry.

Example 13.3 Although fairly rare, dissociative identity disorders have received much public recognition because of books and movies such as *The Three Faces of Eve* and *Sybil*. These cases show how, when faced with anxiety-producing circumstances, an individual switches to another personality that is better able to cope with the situation.

Somatoform Disorders

Symptoms of a physical dysfunction for which no identifiable organic cause can be found indicate a **somatoform disorder**. This differs from **psychosomatic disorders**, which are real physical problems arising, in part, from psychological causes.

A person with minor symptoms who interprets them as evidence of a major illness is showing **hypochondriasis**. When given clearance from medical tests, hypochondriacs often will not accept the results and go to another physician for additional tests.

The term **conversion disorder** comes from the idea that a psychological problem can be converted into a physical problem. Thus, there are symptoms of physical distress, such as paralysis or blindness, for which no organic cause can be found.

Example 13.4 An instructor worried about teaching a large class for the first time awakens to find that she is paralyzed from the waist down. This illustrates conversion disorder. The paralysis means she can no longer be expected to teach the class, and the anxiety is thus reduced.

Mood Disorders

Mood disorders are emotional states that reach levels severe enough to interfere with daily living.

The symptoms of **depressive disorders** include loss of energy, inability to concentrate, agitation, significant weight change, feelings of worthlessness, and thoughts of suicide. **Major depressive disorder** is characterized by periods of great sadness that last 2 weeks or more. **Dysthymia** is a severe form of depression that is chronic. Depression often is linked with **suicide** attempts or actual suicide.

Bipolar disorder is depression accompanied by occasional periods of mania. This consists of a high energy level, increased activity, elation, and expansiveness. The frequency of each state varies, with some people showing a rapid change from mania to depression, others experiencing longer bouts of each, and some interspersing periods of normal behavior between the two extremes.

Schizophrenic Disorders

The group of disorders that includes disturbed thoughts, emotions, and pronounced distortion of or detachment from reality are **schizophrenic disorders**.

 Don't Be Confused!

The term "schizophrenia" is often mistakenly used to refer to dissociative identity disorder.

Disorganized schizophrenia is characterized by a profound disintegration of personality, with frequent **delusions** (irrational beliefs), **hallucinations** (perceptual illusions), inappropriate emotional expressions, and incoherent speech.

Catatonic schizophrenia is indicated by unusual motor patterns. Catatonics show excessive and sometimes violent motor behavior or lapse into an immobility.

Individuals with **paranoid schizophrenia** report delusions of grandeur, persecution, or both. They trust no one and sometimes attempt to retaliate against their supposed persecutors.

The diagnosis of **undifferentiated schizophrenia** means a person shows common schizophrenic symptoms but does not clearly meet the diagnostic criteria of one of the disorders listed above.

Personality Disorders

Personality disorders typically cause more distress for the people around than for the person manifesting the symptoms.

Unconcerned with the rights of others or the rules of society, persons with **antisocial personality disorder** (also called **psychopathic** or **sociopathic**) are not troubled by their actions that bring pain or harm to others. Often charming and bright, they have difficulty forming attachments and typically are manipulative and deceptive.

People with a **narcissistic personality disorder** have an exaggerated sense of self-importance and are likely to seek admiration. They are unlikely to have much regard for others.

Dependent personality disorder is indicated by a lack of self-esteem, responsibility, and a need for others to make important decisions. A person with this type of disorder may lack self-confidence and be extremely sensitive to criticism.

A **paranoid personality disorder** can be thought of as a much less severe form of paranoid schizophrenia. Beliefs associated with persecution are focused on real situations and do not involve delusional or hallucinatory behaviors.

Considerations for Diagnosis of Abnormality

There are **gender differences** in disorder rates. Although there is considerable debate about why this happens, it appears that certain categories are thought to "fit better" with one sex or the other. For example, women are diagnosed with depression more than men, while men are more often diagnosed with antisocial personality disorder.

DSM-IV categories do not necessarily apply to or cover all the circumstances in different **cultures**. Even when the category does seem appropriate, the actual expression of the disorder may be different.

Example 13.5 Symptoms of depression identified in the United States focus on lack of self-esteem and negative affect. In many Asian cultures, depression is identified by somatic (physical) symptoms.

The requirements of the courts in determining **legal insanity** differ from the categories presented in *DSM-IV*. The criteria applied refer to the capacity to distinguish right from wrong or the ability to act in accordance with the law. Several states have instituted a verdict of "guilty but mentally ill."

Solved Problems

Solved Problem 13.1 What is abnormal behavior?

When someone shows behavior noticeably different from the average, it may be called abnormal (away from the norm). This may be of concern when it creates personal discomfort, dysfunction, or difficulties for others.

Solved Problem 13.2 A persistent question is whether certain groups of people are more likely than others to show particular disorders. What has been found in the research?

Gender and culture both relate to the diagnosis of particular disorders, although correlation does not imply causation. Age, marital status, social class, and ethnicity also relate to diagnoses.

Chapter 14
THERAPIES

General Overview of Therapy

The purpose of therapies is to help individuals overcome problems. Therapies can be divided into two major groupings: **biomedical therapies** involve physical or medical procedures; **psychotherapies** are nonmedical technologies. There are varying estimates of the percentage of Americans showing abnormal personality patterns that may require therapy at some time. A

129

fairly agreed upon ratio is one in two, although many do not seek treatment.

There are a number of different types of therapists. Probably the best known are psychiatrists and clinical psychologists. **Psychiatrists** are M.D.s with specialized training. **Clinical psychologists** obtain a Ph.D. or Psy.D. degree. Other types include psychoanalysts, psychiatric nurses, psychiatric social workers, counseling psychologists, and **paraprofessionals**.

There are several trends in treatment that deserve note:

- Many therapists employ **eclectic** approaches, combining different types of therapies.
- Greater use of **psychotropic drugs** has decreased hospitalizations and the length of hospitalizations.
- Greater community involvement has led to the development of **community psychology**. There are now more agencies providing support, resulting in the **deinstitutionalization** of many.
- **Milieu therapy** represents the extension of community values into the hospital setting.

Biomedical Therapies

The most prevalent **biomedical therapy** is **drug therapy**. Two advantages of drug therapies are that (1) there is no tissue destruction and (2) the patient may become more open to therapeutic influence.

Example 14.1 Patients with mood disorders often are treated with drugs (e.g., fluoxetine). It is hoped that the resultant behavior pattern will make the patient more amenable to other forms of treatment.

Also known as **shock therapy**, **electroconvulsive therapy** (**ECT**) involves passing a brief electric current in the range of 70 to 130 volts across the temples. It is believed that ECT may cause the release of the neurotransmitter beta-endorphin, which somehow contributes to relief from severe depression, at least temporarily. ECT may be accompanied by transient memory loss. Today, ECT is used when no other treatment appears viable.

Psychosurgery is surgical removal of brain tissue. **Prefrontal lo-**

botomy involves destroying tissue linking the frontal lobes and the thalamus, with the intent of reducing emotionality and abnormal behaviors. This type of surgery has been abandoned because of the drastic side effects. Current techniques are far more sophisticated, involving the destruction of only very small portions of brain tissue.

Psychodynamic Therapies

The goal of **psychodynamic therapies**, developed by Freud, is for the patient to achieve **insight** into the underlying causes of the abnormal behavior. Techniques used include **free association** (saying whatever comes to mind) and **dream analysis**. Freud distinguished between the **manifest content** of a dream, related to the actual content, and the **latent content**, which held symbolic meaning. To Freud, dreams represented thoughts and wishes the client held but was unable to express consciously. As the crucial causes of the problem come to be expressed, a client often exhibits **resistance**, an unwillingness to discuss the topic. If the resistance can be overcome, the therapy may be successful. As therapy progresses, the client demonstrates **transference**, the development of an emotional relationship with the therapist that mimics the relationship with a parent during childhood. Freud also warned against the possibility of **countertransference**, in which the therapist develops inappropriate affection for the client.

Modern approaches include **ego analysis**, in which there is more of an emphasis on having clients develop adaptive problem-solving skills.

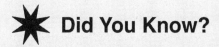 **Did You Know?**

Traditional psychodynamic therapy requires lengthy treatment, sometimes taking years. Some newer psychodynamic approaches attempt to shorten the time required for treatment.

Humanistic Therapies

Humanistic therapy focuses on personal growth or self-actualization. Humanistic therapists believe that problems originate from unreasonable "conditions of worth."

Carl Rogers was the leading advocate of **client-centered therapy**, proposing that a therapist make no judgments about a client's behaviors but instead offer **empathy**, **genuineness**, and **unconditional positive regard**. This is called **nondirective therapy**, with progress depending on the ability of the client to verbalize and work through his or her problems. This therapy works best with clients who are highly verbal.

Gestalt therapy is based on the idea that personality must be treated as an organized whole. A Gestalt therapist encourages a client to gain more control over and become more responsible for his or her actions. The client's aim is to overcome behaviors such as passivity and irresponsibility and to open blocked potentials for growth.

Behavior Therapies

In **behavior therapy** relying on **classical conditioning**, a correctional experience (serving as an unconditioned stimulus) is paired with a conditioned stimulus that appears to provoke maladaptive behavior.

Example 14.2 Systematic desensitization may be used to help overcome fear of the dark. At first the patient may be asked to read stories about dark places. While this occurs, the patient is helped to experience relaxation. Successive steps might include observing a movie about people in caves, actually seeing someone else in a dark room, and finally entering a dark room. Each step pairs relaxation (the new US) with images or experiences of the dark (the CS) until the person is able to confront the dark without feeling intense anxiety.

In **implosion therapy**, the patient imagines the worst possible version of the anxiety-provoking stimulus. In **flooding**, the client is brought in direct contact with the anxiety-provoking situation. **Extinction** and **counterconditioning** are the goals for both implosion and flooding therapies. When the patient once again confronts the anxiety-provoking situation, the memory will be that nothing bad happened and that coping is possible.

Example 14.3 Aversion therapy sometimes is tried with clients who abuse alcohol. By taking a drug that will produce nausea if alcohol is consumed, the client comes to learn that even the slightest use of alcohol will produce very unpleasant reactions.

Operant conditioning techniques concentrate on reinforcing appropriate responses while also extinguishing maladaptive responses. A **token economy** is an application of operant conditioning used mostly in institutional settings. Patients earn or lose tokens as a consequence of their behaviors; the tokens can be traded for privileges or rewards.

In **behavior (contingency) contracting**, the therapist and client establish a contract specifying the behaviors that satisfy the goals of the therapy. The contract includes the behaviors to be rewarded and punished, if necessary.

 **Note!**

It is necessary to be very consistent with behavioral consequences; even an occasional reinforcement for a maladaptive response may make the response resistant to extinction.

The basic principles of **modeling** can be used in therapy. A patient can observe someone coping successfully with an anxiety-provoking situation and imitate the adaptive responses.

Cognitive Therapies

The premise of **cognitive therapies** is that behaviors can be changed if the cognitions underlying those behaviors are changed. Because of this, these therapies are also known as **cognitive-behavioral therapies**.

Developed by **Albert Ellis**, **rational-emotive therapy** helps a client recognize the irrationality of beliefs that control her or his behavior and then practice new ways of thinking and behaving that are more rational.

Example 14.4 A client claims, "I'm no good. I flunked my biology exam." A rational-emotive therapist confronts this irrationality directly by asking, "Why does flunking one exam make you no good?" The client is then given guidance to develop new patterns of responding.

Aaron Beck developed **cognitive therapy**, which aims to help a client learn information that will allow a change from distorted and illogical thinking to patterns that are more logical and adaptive. Cognitive therapy is less confrontational than rational-emotive therapy.

In **Donald Meichenbaum's stress-inoculation therapy**, the client develops an understanding of beliefs associated with stressful situations; acquires and rehearses adaptive, coping self-statements; applies them in the controlled therapy setting; and finally practices and is reinforced for using those strategies in real-life situations.

Group Therapy

In **group therapy**, more than one client is involved in the therapeutic setting at the same time. Groups may include several patients from differing backgrounds or with similar clinical characteristics. The belief is that the group provides a social setting where resolution of problems, which often are first developed in a social setting, may be achieved. A group may provide strong support for the individuals within the group and at the same time exert pressure to change maladaptive behavior. Disadvantages of groups include loss of focus on one's specific problems and less effective responding by the therapist because of the demands created by the group.

Other Concerns with Therapy

Ethical issues are always important in therapy. A therapist is in a position of power that must not be abused. Confidentiality of client information and doing no harm are premises of all therapy.

Therapists must demonstrate **cultural sensitivity** to be effective.

They often must deal with gender, ethnicity, sexual preference, or race as part of the therapeutic process and should be careful to understand the attributes and values associated with these groups.

Many people turn to **self-help** techniques, found in books, in magazines, and on Web sites. Some people report successfully changing their behavior as a result. Whether the program was the reason for this or whether there was **spontaneous remission** of the symptoms or a **placebo effect** is almost impossible to discern.

There is no easy way to determine the **effectiveness of therapy**. Several considerations are important, including the matching of the technique with the symptoms and the expectations of the client and therapist. Nevertheless, most research indicates that a majority of clients claim benefits from therapy.

Chapter 15
SOCIAL
PSYCHOLOGY

Social psychology is the study of the influence of others on the behavior of individuals and groups.

Social Knowledge

Individuals categorize or structure knowledge about the social world using processes similar to those used with other types of knowledge.

A **social category** groups people according to any number of characteristics, such as gender or occupation. **Social schemas** represent feelings and beliefs about social categories. Research has indicated that people tend to seek information that fits with already existing schemas. This is referred to as **confirmatory hypothesis testing**, and in effect it sets the stage for processing subsequent social

knowledge. **Social scripts** are expectancies for behaviors, often tied to specific situations.

Self-schemas contain information about the **self-concept**, the beliefs and feelings people have about themselves. **Self-referencing** refers to situations in which a person is better able to remember something about someone else if that information relates to the self. Thus, one's self-schema is important in affecting the ways one relates to others.

The **self-fulfilling prophecy** is another example of how the self is influenced by others. The behavioral expectations of others can increase the probability that the expected behaviors will occur. When this happens, **behavioral confirmation** is said to have occurred.

Attributions are attempts to explain the causes of behavior that also provide expectations about the future and influence future behaviors. Three dimensions of causal attributions have been studied. The first is whether the behavior can be attributed to an **internal** or an **external** cause. The second is whether the behavior can be attributed to a **stable** or **unstable** cause. Attributions can also be made to **controllable** or **uncontrollable** causes.

Example 15.1 Attributing a good grade on a psychology exam to, "being smart and always doing well no matter what the situation is" provides an example of an internal (smart), stable (always do well), uncontrollable (no matter what) attribution. Attributing the same good grade to, "an easy exam and unusually diligent studying" is an external, unstable, controllable attribution.

There are a number of **attribution biases** that people regularly exhibit. With the **self-serving bias**, attribution for one's successes is made to internal causes, while one's failures are attributed to external causes. **Self-handicapping** also protects the self. It refers to situations where a person creates conditions to prevent successful completion of a task so that there will be an external excuse for failure.

The **fundamental attribution error** is the exaggeration of internal causes for others' behavior, rather than external, situational causes. The **actor-observer bias** is an extension of this. It describes the tendency of people to focus on external causes of their own behavior and internal causes of others' behavior. Both effects probably result from the availability of different types of information about the self and others. Related to the fundamental attribution error is the **correspondence bias**. This is the assumption that people's behaviors correspond to their attitudes and traits. These particular biases are particularly strong in Western cultures.

Example 15.2 Sitting in the residence hall and looking out the window, Alphonse notices a fellow student slip and fall on the sidewalk below. His reaction is, "Look at Roseanne. What a clumsy klutz she is!" When Alphonse leaves for class, he almost falls and immediately responds, "Boy, it's really slippery today!" Alphonse's response reflects both the self-serving bias and the actor-observer bias.

If the initial description of a person is positive, any subsequent interpretation of that person's behavior is likely to be positive, a finding called the **halo effect**. A **negative halo effect** can occur when the initial description is negative.

With the **false consensus bias**, others' characteristics are assumed to match one's own. As a result, what the other does will be interpreted according to one's own beliefs or attitudes, and the other will be expected to act in a manner similar to the self.

Many theorists believe that people wish to maintain **cognitive consistency**, so that the social world appears more predictable. When a person behaves contrary to an important attitude and there is no external justification or attribution for the behavior, **cognitive dissonance** may occur. This is an uncomfortable state that creates a motivation to reduce the dissonance, often by changing the initial attitude to bring it in line with the behavior.

Example 15.3 Cognitive dissonance initially was demonstrated in an experiment in which subjects who were paid $1.00 (low external justification) to tell someone that a boring task was really "fun and interesting." These subjects later changed their attitude and evaluated the task more positively than those who were paid $20.00 (high justification) for telling the same lie.

Attitudes

Attitudes are learned evaluative reactions that are typically thought of as having three components: **affective**, **behavioral**, and **cognitive**.

> # Remember
>
> The ABCs of attitudes are:
>
> - **Affective**: the evaluation of the attitude object
> - **Behavioral**: action toward the attitude object
> - **Cognitive**: beliefs about the attitude object

Attitude formation occurs through classical conditioning, operant conditioning, and modeling.

The study of **attitude change (persuasion)** has identified a number of important variables. Three **source factors** found to be significant are **credibility**, how **attractive** and **likable** the source is, and how much **power** or **prestige** the source has.

A **one-sided argument** appears most effective in solidifying or increasing a favorable attitude if the recipient of a persuasive message is already favorable toward the message. However, if the recipient has a negative attitude, a **two-sided message** may be more effective.

Another consideration is the use of **fear** in a message. Fear-producing messages can be quite effective, as long as the fear evoked is not too strong, in which case the message tends to be ignored. Fear messages also work better when accompanied by specific recommendations about how to avoid the dangerous stimulus.

Being exposed repeatedly to the desired message, person, or attitude object may be enough to positively influence an attitude. This is called the **mere exposure effect**.

The **elaboration-likelihood model** explains the effects of persuasion by reference to how people process information. **Central processing** occurs when messages are carefully examined. Although changing attitude is more difficult to accomplish with central processing, the person will be persuaded by a strong argument and will be likely to sustain the attitude change over time. In contrast, **peripheral processing** does not involve careful examination of the information presented. With peripheral processing, source effects, rather than argument strength effects, are particularly strong.

Prejudice

A **prejudice** is a learned evaluation of members of a social category. Prejudices are developed and maintained in the same way as other learned attitudes. However, modeling may be a particularly important source for learning prejudices, providing an example of the learning that occurs through the process of **socialization**. Occasional support for a prejudice, even when due to confirmatory hypothesis testing, is enough to make the prejudice resistant to extinction.

Stereotypes are overgeneralized beliefs about others that are based on others' membership in social categories or groups.

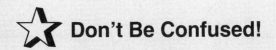 **Don't Be Confused!**

Prejudice is an affect or evaluation.
Discrimination is a behavior.
Stereotypes are beliefs.

These represent the three components of attitudes.

Psychologists make a distinction between **in-groups** (the groups to which one belongs) and **out-groups** (the groups to which others belong). People make different attributions for the behavior of in-groups versus out-groups, demonstrating an **in-group–serving attribution bias**, just like the self-serving attribution bias. People also perceive out-group members as being more similar to one another than in-group members (the **out-group homogeneity effect**) and evaluate and reward out-groups less generously than in-groups. **Social identity theory** is the area of research that accommodates this work.

Interpersonal Attraction

There are many variables that influence **interpersonal attraction**. Even high levels of **arousal**, such as those produced by exercise or an anxiety-provoking situation, lead to greater attraction to an available other met in the aroused state than to a person met in an unaroused state. This is because the arousal is misattributed to the other.

Proximity, the real or perceived distance between one person and another, influences attraction, likely because it provides opportunities for positive interactions.

People with **similar characteristics** often are attracted to each other. This holds for sociological characteristics (socioeconomic status, education), psychological characteristics (attitudes, values), and physical characteristics (height, attractiveness). Similarity provides common ground for interactions and can provide "reinforcement" for the positive evaluation of the self.

Another factor involved in attraction is **physical attractiveness**. People judged to be physically attractive are better liked than are those rated as unattractive. This judgment of attractiveness may cause others to perceive additional positive qualities in the attractive person, which is an example of the **halo effect**.

Example 15.4 The attractiveness of a person may lead others to expect a certain kind of behavior from that person. Thus, if a man is handsome, people may expect him to be charming also. People may perceive charm regardless of whether it actually is one of the man's characteristics because of confirmatory hypothesis testing. Perceivers may also act positively toward the man in ways that elicit charm from him, thus creating a behavioral confirmation of the expectation.

Equity and **exchange theories** suggest that people are attracted to others who "take" at about the same level at which they "give" so that **reciprocity** of benefits is maintained. As relationships develop into what are called **communal relationships**, concerns shift from reciprocity to caring for the needs of the other.

Although **love** is difficult to define, most psychologists view it as representing stronger and deeper feelings than mere attraction. Robert Sternberg has labeled three basic components of love: **intimacy** (closeness, connection), **passion** (physical desire), and **commitment** (desire to sustain the relationship over time). Sternberg proposes that **consummate love** occurs when people are high in all three components. Other types of love result from different combinations of the components. Thus, **infatuated love** is high in passion but low in the other two components, while **companionate love** is low in passion and high in intimacy and commitment.

Group Behavior

Some groups are **formal**, with designated titles and rules. Other groups are **informal**; they are organized casually and have unwritten or flexible rules. Groups also may be **present**, with members actually physically present in the person's environment, or **absent**, which occurs when association with the members is an important influence on behavior even when the group is not physically present.

The presence of others may influence one's performance of a task. If others improve performance, **social facilitation** has taken place. **Social interference** (also called **social inhibition**) occurs when the presence of others impairs performance. Quite frequently, social facilitation will occur when the person is performing a task that is well learned, while social interference may be more likely when the person is performing a task that has not been learned well. This is because of the inverted-U shaped relationship between arousal (caused by the presence of others) and performance.

A person who behaves according to the expectations of a group shows **conformity**. **Nonconformity** is demonstrated by behavior counter to group expectations, while **independence** is behavior that is not influenced by a group. In general, conformity is more likely to occur when the group is attractive to the person being influenced, when the response is public rather than private, when the task is ambiguous, and when the group is unanimous. Conformity is especially reduced when there is even just one ally who advocates a different opinion than that held by the rest of the group.

Example 15.5 Conformity was initially studied by having a subject provide a public estimate of the length of a line after hearing others respond. When the others, who were trained associates of the researcher, all gave the obviously incorrect response, many of the subjects conformed by also supplying the incorrect response.

Compliance is exhibited when behavior is consistent with a direct request. In **obedience**, a person responds to a direct command. Obedience is most likely when the person giving the command is in a position of legitimate authority.

Group dynamics refer to the social interactions that occur within groups. **Group size** affects many social interactions. For example, when a group consists of three people, interactions often create a "two-against-one" situation. Larger groups can produce **diffusion of responsibility**, in which any one person takes less responsibility than he or she would assume if acting alone. One form of this is **social loafing**; this occurs when larger groups produce less than the expected result because each member contributes less than his or her maximum effort to the task. Another form of diffusion is **bystander apathy**. This is relevant to situations in which any one individual is less likely to come to the aid of a victim (**prosocial behavior**) when others are present, apparently assuming that the others will act.

Aggression may be explained by a number of factors. The psychoanalytic view is that aggression is instinctual and occurs as an attempt to achieve **catharsis**, a release of built-up aggressive tendencies. A second view is that aggression results from experiencing frustration. Social learning theory emphasizes the importance of learning aggressive behaviors from models. It is this latter theory that has received the most research support.

Group polarization occurs when groups make more extreme decisions than any one member of the group would make if acting alone. An extreme version of group polarization is **groupthink**. The group atmosphere is such that members believe that the group's opinions are invulnerable to criticism (an **illusion of invulnerability**). Apparent unanimity of the members' opinions convinces them of their inherent rightness, in spite of evidence to the contrary. Opposing evidence may be ignored, and dissenters may be urged to change their views to conform with those of the group.

Note!

The surprise attack on Pearl Harbor by Japan, the Cuban Bay of Pigs disaster, and the space shuttle Challenger explosion have all been attributed to flawed reasoning as a result of groupthink.

Sometimes groups elicit behavior that would never occur when individuals acted alone. This is due to a loss of individuality and a reduction of normative constraints against unacceptable behaviors; it has been termed **deindividuation**. Although deindividuation often involves negative forms of social behavior, more positive responses can result from this state if the group norm favors positive behavior.

Solved Problems

Solved Problem 15.1 Mitchell is a bright child. He has been encouraged by his teachers to pursue special art training, being told: "You're really a good 'drawer.' You can be a great artist." What principle describes why, if Mitchell hears such remarks, he will be likely to show success in the field of art?

Psychologists explain Mitchell's situation by referring to the self-fulfilling prophecy, in which the expectations of others can influence behavior. The more Mitchell hears people endorse his skills, the more likely it is that he will work hard, set high goals for himself, and therefore perform well. His resulting excellent work will provide behavioral confirmation of the expectations.

Solved Problem 15.2 Standing on the first tee, Sandy complains about the "horrible work schedule" that has kept him from practicing for the last two weeks. "I probably have no chance to play well," he says. How do Sandy's comments relate to self-handicapping?

Self-handicapping refers to situations where a person creates conditions that work against successful performance. It may be that Sandy intentionally planned a busy work schedule to provide a ready excuse for not playing well.

Index